ACT THERAPY WORKBOOK FOR ADULTS

An Easy-to-Read (No Jargon!) Acceptance & Commitment Therapy
Guide for Mindfulness and Mental Wellness

—

Overcome Anxiety, Panic Attacks, Depression
& Shame with Practical Exercises

LIFEZEN PUBLICATIONS

ISBN 9789083397429 (Paperback)
ISBN 9789083397436 (Hardback)

A Gift to Our Readers!

Jumpstart your healing journey with our free ACT Mini Guide (incl. 21-Day Self-Guided ACT Plan!).

Just go to https://life-zen.com/guides/act or scan the QR code on this page.

Plus, unlock a *special bonus* just for you!

Table of Contents

Introduction

"I. Struggle." – Ava Walters

Every day felt like an endless emotional struggle. I don't remember exactly how it started. I was just always "coping" until I wasn't anymore.

No one knew about it, of course. Every single day, I would put on a brave face and a very "put-together" attitude. At work, people looked up to me for guidance. Friends routinely confided their troubles with me, seeking my opinion or advice. My parents would call me if my younger twin brothers needed more "guidance," my brothers would seek me out whenever they needed a buffer between them and our parents. Ha! If only they all knew how lost I was inside.

> *Later, with therapy, I would realize that my life was this constant cycle of being pulled by different people in different directions. I was always "someone" to someone... but I was never just me. I was never Ava to Ava.*

My husband and I have a great relationship now. But it was a rocky start, a very rocky start. During those early years, I felt I had to "lead." In my head, nothing happens if I don't discuss them, plan them, or address them. Even something as simple as date nights became an issue.

Me: We need to go out and spend some alone time together.
Hubby: Okay. Great.

Me: That's it? Why do I have to think and plan these things? Why do I have to do everything?!

Of course, an argument would follow. Actually, it was often a one-sided argument because I would huff and puff, and my husband would either let me be, try to calm me down, or just give in.

One day, we got into more or less the same argument, and I ended up with the same statements. This time, though, my husband stopped me dead in my tracks.

Me: Why do I have to do everything?!
Hubby: Honey, when will you realize you don't have to?
Me: What the hell do you mean?
Hubby: You think of something and want it addressed NOW and YOUR WAY. You don't give me time to think, give my opinion, or share my plans. You do the same at work until you're all stressed and worn out.

I was rendered speechless. I kept staring at my husband, and he kept looking calmly at me, never breaking eye contract. He wasn't daring me. He was giving me time to process. Looking back, I must have looked like a cartoon character in front of him, a myriad of emotions fleeting over my face. In the end, all I could say was...

Me: Why didn't you tell me your opinion before?
Hubby: Well, during those moments, you already look... frazzled like a busy, stressed bee. I didn't think it was the time to address it. I felt it would make you even more anxious.
Me: You mean it was easier for YOU to handle it that way!
Hubby: Maybe. But...
Me: What?!

Hubby: Well, I didn't want to end up in a bigger fight like the one you're trying to pick right now.

I was rendered speechless—again.

It would be great to say things got all better and rosy afterward. It didn't. People can't just "pivot" from who they are or how they have been living life overnight. So, what changed for me? I hit rock bottom.

You see, stress, anxiety, and deep and difficult emotions don't just flow in and out of you without leaving anything behind. Little by little, situation by situation, year by year... these struggles wear you down. For me, the weight of desperately trying to juggle multiple responsibilities and taking on more and more without ever pausing to catch my breath broke me.

One day, as I sat at my desk at work, surrounded by a mountain of unfinished tasks, I felt a sudden wave of panic wash over me. My heart raced, my palms grew clammy, but I felt oddly cold inside. I stared at one fixed point and tried desperately to bring my breath back to a normal rhythm.

When I succeeded, I moved on as if nothing happened. Later that night, I silently asked myself if that was a panic attack... and then I brushed it off. However, as the days turned into weeks and the weeks into months, I found myself experiencing the same thing again and again, with no relief.

At one point, the company I worked for decided to send me overseas for three months. (As a Project Manager by profession, this wasn't unusual; I've done it several times before.) This time, though, things were different.

During the first week I was overseas, I had a mild panic attack, but this time, I felt an enormous dark cloud loom over me. The panic attack decreased, but the dark cloud of gloom stayed with me. Then, one day, as I returned to the hotel where I was staying and entered my room, I just started crying—big, fat, ugly tears. I couldn't stop, and I felt myself unraveling. From that moment on, every single day was a struggle stronger than the day before. Somehow, I survived the three months and returned home, but I wasn't the same.

In addition to the random panic attacks, I felt immensely sad, incredibly alone, often confused, and just bone-deep tired. I attributed the first week to bad jet lag and the second to life, work responsibilities, and pressure. But, when I was still feeling physically and emotionally exhausted by the end of the month, something inside me knew I needed help. I was struggling, and I didn't know what to do.

I met with a therapist, and over our sessions, we concluded that I was suffering from what I now call "a breakdown and a burnout." And this condition stemmed from my relentless people-pleasing and controlling tendencies.

People came to "me" for help when they needed something, which gave me self-worth. It was the only gasoline for my self-esteem. I'm good as long as I was needed and looked like I've got it all together.

Of course, my fears of being found out as "not good enough" and that, in truth, "I don't belong here" developed my need for control. (Yes, that's imposter syndrome.)

Over the years, I became consumed with controlling every aspect of my life to ensure I could dictate the outcome. This constant need for control only served to heighten my stress and anxiety. Eventually, I reached a point where I couldn't keep up anymore. My mind and body were exhausted from the constant juggling, coping, and controlling. I ran out of gas.

I'm extremely grateful for undergoing therapy. It helped me understand what I was going through, but sometimes, I felt like it wasn't addressing my specific issues. I felt something missing, as though I was seeing a glimpse of something, but I could not take the next meaningful step forward. So, I concluded my sessions and set out on my own. After some research, I came across Dialectical Behavior Therapy (DBT) by Dr. Marsha Linehan.

As I became more familiar with DBT, I discovered the powerful concept of acceptance (specifically, *Radical Acceptance*), and this proved to be my turning point. Acceptance was the key I've been looking for to unlock me from the cage of my mental and emotional struggles.

Acceptance is so simple, so powerful, yet oh so misunderstood!

You might think, "Acceptance alone won't solve my problems. It doesn't change my circumstances." You know what? You're right. Acceptance isn't the final destination but the necessary starting point for your healing journey. It is what you need to do to *allow* movement from point A to point B.

After discovering the benefits of DBT and taking Dr. Linehan's DBT Skills certificate course, I immersed myself in other types of behavior therapy, including Cognitive Behavioral Therapy (CBT) and Acceptance and Commitment Therapy (ACT).

While these three approaches share many similarities, there are also distinct differences. DBT emphasizes mental and emotional skills training and validation,

CBT focuses on identifying and challenging negative thought patterns, and ACT emphasizes acceptance and values-based action.

This book serves as a compassionate guide specifically focused on navigating the principles and practices of ACT. Why? I believe that truly experiencing the life you want should be based on your values, not the ones dictated by society or others. This was crucial to my mental healing, and I hope it does the same for you.

When I started my journey, I only wanted to "feel better." I never thought I would be radically transformed! It's a bit hard to explain, really. It's like I was going through life, seeing everything in muted colors and carrying this constant weight on my shoulders.

After ACT, my relationship with myself, my husband, other family members, and my outlook in life in general dramatically improved. **I wasn't just feeling better; I was happy.** And you know the thing about happiness, right? It has this tendency to radiate outwards.

Soon, people who knew about my troubles asked me what I had done to turn my life around. I started sharing my journey, and as more and more people reached out, I realized that the best way to live my life was to do my best to pay what I learned forward.

So, dear reader, this book is my personal invitation to you to go on a journey of deep self-discovery and healing with me.

I have been where you are. I know what you're going through. It would be my deepest honor to be of any kind of help to you right now. I offer you the kind of help I desperately needed and received back then.

Who Should Read This Book

This book is for anyone who is struggling right now or wants to support someone who is struggling. Perhaps you're considering therapy but prefer to start with something at home, or you just haven't found the right therapist yet. Maybe you're already in therapy and seek additional support. Regardless, **this book is for you if you want answers and relief**.

How This Book is Different

This book is your modern-day guide to Acceptance and Commitment Therapy (ACT) and how it can help you move from where you are to where you want to be. However, this book takes a rather uncommon perspective in that I've included some elements of Dialectical Behavior Therapy (DBT) and Cognitive Behavioral Therapy (CBT). I've found them to be extremely helpful in my healing journey, and I hope they benefit you, too.

How to Use This Workbook

The chapters in this book build on one another. So please start at the beginning and work your way through.

Also, I firmly believe that learning is knowledge + action. It's not enough to know something; you need to apply it for that knowledge to be useful. That's why each chapter provides guided exercises. As you accomplish each worksheet, you gain a deeper understanding of the concepts discussed and actively integrate them into your life. This integration is where the real transformation happens. It's like learning to swim by jumping into the water rather than just reading about it on dry land.

The Power of YOU

Please don't underestimate yourself. Humans are resilient creatures, so know that you have a remarkable ability to adapt, learn, and evolve in the face of adversity. You CAN break free from mental and emotional suffering and transform.

Also, whatever you're experiencing right now, know that **your truth matters**. Your feelings are valid. Your experiences are relevant, and your struggles deserve attention. Please don't let anyone undercut your reality or your voice. You have the right to feel what you feel and take the time to heal.

Speaking of healing, please always extend kindness and patience with yourself because this will not be a linear process. There will be ups and downs, but I promise you: You'll always be going forward if you stick with the process.

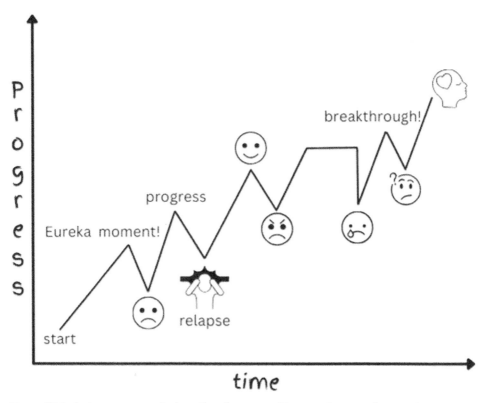

Note: This is just a sample healing journey. You and your circumstances are unique, so yours will most likely look different. Wouldn't it be amazing to discover your own unique path to healing?

Ava Watters

Amazon Bestselling Author
Acceptance Therapy Advocate

Part 1: Acceptance and Commitment Therapy 101

"Accept yourself, love yourself, and keep moving forward. If
you want to fly, you have to give up what weighs you down."
– Roy T. Bennett

Chapter 1: What is Acceptance and Commitment Therapy?

Acceptance and Commitment Therapy (ACT) was developed in the late 1980s by psychologist Steven C. Hayes[1] and his colleagues as they were working with people struggling with psychological problems such as anxiety and depression. (Hayes himself is no stranger to anxiety and has, over the years, talked openly about his panic disorder and experience with panic attacks.)

ACT draws from *behaviorism*, which emphasizes the influence of our environment and learning experiences on our behavior. It also incorporates elements of *Cognitive Behavioral Therapy (CBT)* and *Behavioral Therapy*, which focus on modifying maladaptive or unhelpful behavior.

For example, imagine Sarah. As a child, she was bitten by a dog, leading her to fear and thus avoid encountering dogs from that moment on. This avoidant behavior never left her. The thing is, as an adult, Sarah is very much into health and fitness and would love to try running. However, her fear of dogs prevents her from doing this because she fears potentially meeting a dog during a run.

In the above example, behaviorism highlights how Sarah came to fear dogs. By applying CBT and Behavioral Therapy techniques, Sarah might overcome this fear by exploring evidence that not all dogs are dangerous.

Now, you might say this solves Sarah's problems. But that's not entirely true. If you think about it, the above example illustrates a *before-and-after* situation. "Before" is Sarah being afraid of dogs, while "after" is her no longer afraid of them. But what about "during?" How can Sarah address the *exact moments* she's experiencing fear in front of a dog? This is where ACT comes in.

ACT goes beyond traditional behavioral and cognitive therapy approaches by incorporating acceptance- and mindfulness-based strategies to help individuals develop *psychological flexibility.*

Psychological flexibility is similar to the *bamboo principle.* Like the sturdy bamboo tree, you should be capable of bending or adapting to whatever life throws at you (e.g., difficult thoughts, unpleasant emotions, bad experiences, etc.) – without breaking. Or, at the very least, you should be able to bend or adapt to the point that you relieve yourself from mental and emotional suffering.

ACT believes a person lacking psychological flexibility struggles to adapt to life's challenges and may feel stuck or overwhelmed by difficult emotions or situations.

For example, someone with low psychological flexibility will most likely find coping with change or uncertainty challenging. They may become overly anxious or avoidant when faced with new experiences, challenges, or the unexpected, making navigating life's ups and downs difficult. This inflexibility can lead to increased stress, decreased resilience, and overall dissatisfaction and unhappiness with life. How? Well, let's go back to "Sarah."

Imagine that Sarah is happy where she currently lives because she lives in a pet-free apartment building with hardly any dogs in her neighborhood. But what if a great work opportunity comes along that requires her to relocate? If she has low psychological flexibility, she might not dare to leave her current surroundings and comfort zone. What if she meets a friend or potential partner who loves dogs and lives with one? Sarah might avoid all of these potentially great relationships. One day, she might wake up and feel unfulfilled and unhappy with her life.

Now, you might say the above story is farfetched. But, is it?

Humans are hardwired to avoid the things they don't like, fear, or anything that causes unpleasant or negative emotions.[2] The problem with avoidance is that the trigger is never addressed, so you will almost always think, feel, and behave the same way when encountering it. And the more you do it, over time, what (or who) you're avoiding ends up controlling you.

Psychological flexibility is about being open and accepting of your thoughts and feelings–even the really difficult ones–without letting them rule your life. It means:

1. **You can adapt to "change," "different," or the "unexpected."** Psychological flexibility means you can easily adjust to life's ups and downs. It's about rolling with the punches and coping when things don't go as planned.

2. **You can face challenges that come your way.** Psychological flexibility encourages you to acknowledge difficult thoughts and feelings instead of avoiding or ignoring them. It's like saying, "Okay, I feel really anxious right now, but that's okay. I can handle it."

3. **You are present in the moment.** Psychological flexibility involves mindfulness and awareness of what's happening right now. Instead of worrying about the past or future, it's about staying grounded and focused on the present.

4. **You can choose your actions.** Even when dealing with tough emotions, psychological flexibility helps you focus on what's important. It's about choosing actions that align with your values and life goals, even if it's hard or uncomfortable.

5. **You don't need to be in control.** Sometimes, trying to control everything only makes things worse. Psychological flexibility teaches you to let go of the need for control and accept uncertainty. Instead of being fearful and uncomfortable, you're okay with the unknown and curious about what may happen.

So, psychological flexibility is like having the mental and emotional agility to navigate life's twists and turns with grace and resilience. Great! But is ACT for you? Studies have shown that ACT has many applications across various aspects of life and can help with the following:

1. **Improves mental health.** ACT is effective in treating various mental health issues, including anxiety[3,4], depression[5], PTSD[6,7], OCD[8,9],

and substance abuse[10,11]. It helps individuals develop healthy coping skills to manage their symptoms and improve their well-being.

2. **Reduces stress.**[12,13] ACT teaches mindfulness and acceptance techniques to help individuals cope with stress more effectively. By learning to accept difficult thoughts and feelings and focus on the present moment, people can reduce their stress levels and improve their resilience.

3. **Helps with chronic pain management.**[14,15] ACT is effective in helping individuals cope with chronic pain conditions. By changing their relationship to pain and focusing on value-centric actions, people can improve their quality of life and function better despite pain. (Important: This is not about denying the existence of pain. It's modifying how one relates to pain.)

4. **Boosts work and performance.**[16,17] ACT principles can be applied to enhance performance and productivity in various areas of life, including work, sports, and academics. By clarifying values, setting goals, and taking committed action in line with these values, individuals can achieve their full potential and overcome obstacles that may hinder their success.

5. **Improves relationships.**[18,19] ACT can improve communication and interpersonal skills, leading to healthier and more satisfying relationships. By cultivating acceptance and how to extend empathy and compassion to others, people can strengthen connections and build better relationships with others.

6. **Life transitions.**[20] ACT can be beneficial during major life transitions, such as career changes, relationship changes, or loss. By focusing on values

and taking purposeful action, individuals can navigate these transitions with greater clarity and resilience.

7. **Personal growth.**[21,22] Even for those without specific mental health concerns, ACT can be valuable for personal growth and self-discovery. By increasing self-awareness, clarifying values, and fostering mindfulness, individuals can lead more authentic and fulfilling lives.

As you can see, the applications of ACT are diverse. To be honest, I don't see anyone not benefiting from ACT. Our world right now is full of chaos and uncertainty, and stress levels all across the globe are at an all-time high.[23] So, in my opinion, we all need more psychological flexibility, don't you think?

Chapter 2: Successful ACT Therapy at Home

ACT is usually done with a qualified therapist. The number of sessions depends on the nature and severity of the issues being addressed and your goals. However, most individuals see benefits within a relatively short period, often ranging from 6 to 20 sessions.[24,25] (This assumes active engagement between the therapist and the client.) This doesn't mean, though, that self-guided, at-home ACT is not possible.

For self-guided ACT to be successful, approach it with an open mind, a commitment to practice, and a willingness to explore your thoughts, emotions, and behaviors. Don't worry; the following chapters will explain and guide you every step of the way!

Before we begin, let's start with a few exercises to give you a great starting point for your self-guided ACT practice.

Have you ever stepped into a place and immediately felt a sense of peace, calm, or safety wash over you? Perhaps it wasn't the physical space itself but rather a particular item, scent, or memory associated with it that brought you back to a pleasant moment in time.

Our sensory experiences hold incredible power to influence our emotions and state of mind.[26] So, as you embark on this journey of healing and self-discovery, I highly encourage you to begin by creating your own sanctuary—a place where you can retreat during moments of distress or uncertainty.

You can call it your "safe space," your "happy place," or simply your "sanctuary." Whatever resonates with you, the purpose remains the same: to establish a physical or mental refuge where you can find solace, clarity, and peace amidst life's challenges.

Exercise 1: Physical Safe Space

It's important to carve a space for yourself for your healing journey. This physical safe space can provide a dedicated environment to engage in ACT activities, reflection, and self-care practices. Here's how you can create a physical safe space for self-therapy:

1. **Pick a quiet and private area** in your home where you feel relaxed and safe. This could be a corner of a room, a cozy nook, or a specific chair or cushion where you can sit comfortably.

2. **Remove any clutter or distractions** from the space to create a clean and organized environment. Minimize visual and auditory distractions that could disrupt your focus during therapy sessions.

3. **Create a calming atmosphere** by adjusting the lighting, temperature, and overall "feel" of the space. Use soft lighting, candles, or natural light to create a soothing environment. Consider adding comforting elements such as cushions, blankets, or plants.

4. **Personalize the space** by adding personal touches and meaningful items. Display photographs, artwork, or objects that evoke happy or positive emotions or memories for you. Add elements that reflect your interests, values, and personality to make the space inviting and supportive.

5. **Add therapeutic tools and resources** that support your self-therapy practice. For example, place your journals, notebooks, pens, mindfulness exercises, relaxation techniques, self-help books, or any other resources that resonate with you here.

6. **Set boundaries** to protect your safe space and maintain its integrity. Inform family members about the importance of respecting your privacy during your therapy sessions. Use physical cues such as closing the door and hanging a "do not disturb" sign to signal your engagement in self-therapy activities. (Important: Respect your own boundary by not bringing your mobile phone inside your safe space. If you must, put it on silent or allow only specific numbers to go through.)

7. Before engaging in any self-therapy session, **take a few moments to ground yourself** in the present moment. If you just "dive in" to therapy, you might find yourself resisting, especially if you're having a long and stressful day. As such, it's best if you can center yourself first. Just breathe

deeply for a minute, and with each exhale, imagine yourself moving away from everything and closer to your healing practice.

8. **Establish a routine** to maintain consistency and momentum. Schedule a dedicated time in your calendar for reading this book, carrying out the exercises, self-care and reflection, etc.

9. After each self-guided ACT session, **take time to reflect** on your experiences and insights. Write in a journal about your thoughts, feelings, and observations, and consider any actions or adjustments you want to make moving forward.

10. **Extend patience and kindness to yourself.** Be gentle and compassionate with yourself as you navigate your self-therapy journey. Embrace imperfection and allow yourself to experiment, learn, and grow, knowing that your safe space is always available for calmness, healing, and self-discovery.

Exercise 2: Mental Safe Space

A dedicated physical safe space you can go to for healing is great, but what if you're experiencing anxiety, distress, or any other unpleasant emotion and you can't access this space? This is where a mental safe space comes in. It's a dedicated room inside your mind to access anytime you need comfort and relief.

1. **Find a quiet and comfortable space** where you won't be disturbed.

2. Take a few deep breaths to **center yourself** and bring your focus to the present moment.

3. Close your eyes and **imagine yourself in a serene and peaceful environment**. This could be a place from your past, a favorite vacation spot, or an imaginary location.

4. **Use your senses to fully immerse yourself in this mental space.** Notice the sights, sounds, smells, and textures around you. Visualize the details of the environment, such as the colors, shapes, and patterns.

   One by one, focus on each of your senses:

   - **Sight**: Visualize the scenery around you. What do you want to see in your safe space? What will bring your calmness and assurance? Are there any specific colors, objects, or landscapes you connect to these positive emotions?
   - **Sound**: Listen to the sounds in your safe space. Are there birds chirping, waves crashing, or gentle breezes rustling?
   - **Smell**: Imagine any pleasant scents in the air. It could be the aroma of flowers, the freshness of the ocean, the earthy smell of the forest, the favorite scent of a loved one, etc.
   - **Touch**: Feel the textures around you. Are you sitting on soft grass, walking on warm sand, or resting against a smooth tree trunk?
   - **Taste**: If applicable, imagine the taste of any food or drink that might be present in your mental safe space. It could be a refreshing fruit, a comforting beverage, or any other favorite treat.

5. After establishing your mental safe space, **slowly open your eyes and take a moment to ground yourself in the present moment**. Reflect on how it felt to create and immerse yourself in this safe space. Notice any shifts in your mood, mindset, or overall well-being.

Remember that your mental safe space is ALWAYS available whenever you need it. You can return to it anytime you feel stressed, anxious, or overwhelmed.

Exercise 3: Kindness Mantras

It would be great if you could get into the habit of entering your physical and mental safe spaces, even during times when you don't need them. For example, when I wake up, I like to take a moment, close my eyes again, and go into my mental safe space for a minute or two. I find that it gives me a little "morning happy boost."

However, you would likely want to enter these safe spaces because you're going through moments of pain, worries, or stress. In these instances, you might encounter resistance. You might say, "I don't have time for this!" or "Why am I doing this?!"

I ask you to take a deep breath and be kind to yourself during these moments. Following is a list of mantras that might help you. Please feel free to write your own, too.

- I will take this time and offer compassion to myself.
- This is me being kind to myself in times of struggle and pain.
- I am resisting. This is okay. This is normal. I'm going to breathe in kindness and exhale resistance now.
- I will take this time to give myself gentleness and understanding.
- I have a heart of kindness and will channel that to myself now.
- I deserve this safe and calming moment.

Exercise 4: I Want...

This exercise aims to help you establish your intention with your ACT practice. It's important to clearly define what you hope to achieve to have a clearer roadmap for your therapeutic journey. Plus, writing down your intentions can serve as a commitment to yourself.

Important: If you can't list 10 things, that's okay. If you want to write more down, that's fine too. What's important is that you get CLARITY about yourself, your current situation, and what you want for yourself.

Also, please remember that it's normal to see your priorities change (i.e., something you may want right now might turn out to be something unimportant later). As such, you may want to revisit this exercise and do it again later. Now, let's get to the exercise.

Step 1: Write down 10 or more things YOU WANT.

Example: I want to wake up energized and optimistic about my day.

1. _____
2. _____
3. _____
4. _____
5. _____
6. _____
7. _____
8. _____
9. _____
10. _____

Step 2: Write down 10 or more things YOU DON'T WANT.

Example: I don't want to constantly compare myself to my co-worker.

    1. _____

    2. _____

    3. _____

    4. _____

    5. _____

    6. _____

    7. _____

    8. _____

    9. _____

    10. _____

Step 3: Take your DON'T WANT list, and write down what you WANT INSTEAD.

Example:

DON'T WANT: I don't want to constantly compare myself to my co-worker.

WANT INSTEAD: I want to appreciate my unique strengths and abilities without measuring myself against others.

    1. _____

    2. _____

    3. _____

    4. _____

    5. _____

    6. _____

    7. _____

    8. _____

    9. _____

    10. _____

Part 2: The Six Core Principles of ACT

"The secret of change is to focus all of your energy, not on fighting the old, but on building the new."— Socrates

The main objective of ACT is to enhance your *psychological flexibility*, which can be achieved by practicing *Acceptance*, *Mindfulness*, *Cognitive Defusion*, *Self as Context*, *Values Clarification*, and *Committed Action*.

Acceptance in ACT means acknowledging and embracing your thoughts, emotions, and experiences–without trying to avoid, change, or judge them. It's acknowledging that happiness and sadness both exist in this world. For example, on Monday, you might be bursting with happiness. On Tuesday, you might experience sorrow and pain. Acceptance is acknowledging the Mondays and Tuesdays of life.

Mindfulness involves being fully present and aware of your thoughts, feelings, bodily sensations, and the world around you in the present moment. It's about observing your experiences without judgment or attachment, fostering a sense of clarity and insight.

Cognitive Defusion is about learning techniques to detach yourself from unhelpful thoughts and beliefs by recognizing them as just that–thoughts. They are not facts or rules to live by.

Self as Context in ACT is the "observing self." It's that part of you that notices what you're seeing, doing, saying, and thinking. For example, say you're eating your favorite ice cream flavor. (Mine's pistachio, by the way.) The "engaged self" in this activity is your mouth. The "observing self" is that part of you noticing how much pleasure you get from eating that scoop of ice cream.

Values Clarification represents what matters most to you: your deepest desires, aspirations, and guiding principles. I believe that one of the most common reasons for unhappiness today is that we don't take the time to identify our core values or have drifted so far away from them as the years go by. In ACT, clarifying your values helps you identify the kind of person you want to be and the life you want to live, guiding your choices and actions accordingly.

Committed Action involves taking purposeful steps towards living a life aligned with your values. (No more living based on other people's opinions, wishes, and standards.) It's about setting goals that reflect your values and actively working towards them, even in the face of challenges or discomfort.

These six core principles are interconnected, working together to promote psychological flexibility. In the following chapters, you'll dive deep into these concepts and strengthen your "mental bamboo."

Reminder: The best way to benefit from ACT is to practice its fundamental principles *before* you need them. So, learn them, practice them often, and be proficient in them. If you do, they'll come to your rescue whenever you need them.

Chapter 3: Acceptance

In the context of ACT, acceptance means being open to experiencing all of your thoughts, feelings, sensations, and memories without judgment, avoidance, or criticism.

When we're happy, it's easy to bask in the experience and prolong that feeling of happiness. However, when we encounter something (or someone) that triggers unpleasant or difficult emotions, we want to shut the door at them!

But here's the thing: shutting the door on difficult emotions does not eliminate them. Now, you can choose to stay "inside," but isn't that limiting your world? Isn't that letting life's problems and difficulties control you? Instead, why not try acceptance?

Imagine acceptance as opening the door to life's difficult, negative, and unpleasant experiences–and acknowledging their existence without judgment or resistance.

You accept not because you're "okay" with problems and hardships but because you recognize that they are part of the human experience. No single person in the world is always happy and never has problems. And there's nobody who's always into doom and gloom and never ever smiles. Even people suffering from depression or other mental health conditions have likely experienced moments of happiness.[27]

Why Is It So Hard to Accept?

Acceptance is easier said than done. Sure, the word itself is familiar, but in reality, most people misunderstand the concept, and that's why it's sometimes hard to apply. Here are some of the most common roadblocks to acceptance:

1. **Avoidance.** One of the biggest roadblocks to acceptance is the tendency to avoid or suppress difficult thoughts, emotions, or situations. For example, when you feel anxious about a challenging conversation, you might avoid it altogether rather than face it head-on. This avoidance may provide temporary relief, but it ultimately prolongs suffering by preventing true acceptance and processing of these experiences.

2. **Fear of Emotions.** You might fear experiencing certain emotions, especially ones you consider negative or uncomfortable. For instance, you might suppress feelings of sadness because you're scared of being overwhelmed by them.

3. **Attachment to Control.** Another roadblock to acceptance is the desire for control over outcomes or circumstances. For example, when faced with unexpected changes in your plans, you might get stressed or anxious and try to micromanage every detail to regain a sense of control. In your mind, "unknown" might result in "bad."

4. **Judgment and Self-Criticism.** You frequently judge yourself harshly and hold yourself to unrealistic standards. For instance, if you make a mistake at work, you might berate yourself for being incompetent instead of accepting that everyone makes errors occasionally. These internal criticisms may fuel self-doubt and even anxiety and depression.[28]

5. **Rumination and Overthinking.** Constantly dwelling on past events or worrying about the future can prevent acceptance of the present moment. Rumination and overthinking keep the mind stuck in loops of repetitive thoughts, making it difficult to let go and fully engage with reality as it is. For example, you might replay a past argument in your mind repeatedly, analyzing every word said and imagining different outcomes.

6. **Social Influences.** External pressures and societal norms can also contribute to roadblocks to acceptance. For example, if you see your friends achieving certain milestones, you might feel inadequate or inferior because you haven't reached the same level of success.

7. **Lack of Awareness.** You may not realize that you're resisting acceptance because you're so accustomed to your habitual patterns of thinking and behavior. For example, you might not recognize that your tendency to downplay your emotions hinders your ability to accept and address them effectively.

8. **Confusion About the Meaning of Acceptance.** Most people associate acceptance with "I agree" or "I forgive." This is not what acceptance means. Let me clarify this further.

- **Acceptance doesn't mean you're okay or agreeing with something.** In truth, you're not agreeing to anything! You're just acknowledging the existence of a situation, the prevalence of certain emotions, etc. For example, say you and your partner are having an argument. In this scenario, accept that you disagree with each other and that this disagreement is causing you sadness. This practice of acceptance does not equal agreeing with what your partner is saying.

- **Acceptance is not denying something happened.** You're not trying to deny or avoid difficult situations or negative feelings here. You're accepting your awareness of them so you can find healthy ways to cope.

- **Acceptance is not giving up or giving in.** Accepting doesn't mean you don't want things to improve or are okay with it happening again. For example, suppose a friend stood you up for a long-awaited dinner engagement. In this case, accept the fact that your friend stood you up. In the future, set boundaries with this friend for better communication and reliability. Acceptance allows you to acknowledge the reality of the situation without dwelling on negative emotions or becoming consumed by resentment.

- **Acceptance is not about downplaying or trivializing.** Acceptance does not underestimate or undervalue anything. In contrast, it promotes full and unwavering acceptance of challenging or distressing experiences.

For example, *I am in pain here. I acknowledge this feeling. I have a right to feel this now.*

- **Acceptance doesn't mean "I lose."** Many people think acceptance means they're wrong (and thus, someone else is right). Acceptance is not about win or lose, or wrong or right. Acceptance is simply acknowledging facts and reality.

At this stage, I'd like to introduce you to a concept I learned while undergoing Dialectical Behavior Therapy (DBT): **Radical Acceptance**.

In my opinion, Radical Acceptance goes just one small step further than ACT's Acceptance concept because it simplifies the principle while simultaneously pushing you to practice complete and unwavering acceptance.

In my experience, Radical Acceptance is one of the most freeing concepts I've ever encountered because it teaches us not to fight reality but simply to accept reality AS IS.

It's unnecessary to think, evaluate, or analyze a situation that has already happened. You cannot go back in time and re-do it, right? So, the best thing you can do is to accept the reality that it happened.

You don't need to overthink or criticize your feelings or reactions to something or someone either. For example, you're anxious about an upcoming event at work. You cannot just click "Close" on emotions, right? The best thing you can do is accept the reality that you're feeling anxious.

Here's a very simple and effective illustration of what Radical Acceptance is all about.

R A D I C A L   A C C E P T A N C E

IT'S RAINING!   IT'S RAINING!

No......!
It's going to be a gloomy day.
Well, I can't do any of my plans now.
Why is this happening to me?
When will this rain end?!   *Yep!*
My day's ruined!
It's always raining. I hate this place.
This is so unfair!

www.life-zen.com

The above image shows how "marinating" or spending so much time thinking about the rain prolongs your suffering. In contrast, accepting that it is raining allows you to move on faster!

Hello dear reader,

Would you like to explore Radical Acceptance further? If you do, I invite you to get the Amazon bestseller "The Radical Acceptance Workbook: Transform Your Life & Free Your Mind with the Healing Power of Self-Love & Compassion — Positive Lessons to Treat Anxiety, Self-Doubt, Shame & Negative Self-Judgement."

Just visit https://life-zen.com/rad-acceptance or scan this QR code.

Now that we've delved into the complexities of acceptance and cleared up any misconceptions, I hope you're ready to practice acceptance. Here's a quick rundown of how acceptance can benefit your life.

- **Reduces mental and emotional suffering.** Imagine acceptance as this one big "Letting Go" sign. You're letting go of overthinking; you're letting go of control over situations beyond your influence; you're releasing yourself from the grip of uncomfortable and painful emotions. You don't need to suffer from your emotional and mental burdens. You can accept them and, in doing so, reduce their impact on you.

- **Builds resilience.** Acceptance builds emotional resilience by allowing you to move through difficult situations with greater ease and inner power.

- **Enhances emotional regulation.** Acceptance fosters healthier coping mechanisms by encouraging you to respond to emotions with compassion and understanding rather than avoidance or suppression.

THE ACT THERAPY WORKBOOK FOR ADULTS

- **Reduces stress.** Accepting the present moment AS IS can alleviate stress by reducing the need to control difficult circumstances. For example, suppose a friend's birthday is coming up, and you're stressed about seeing an ex-mutual friend during the birthday party. By radically accepting that your ex-friend will be there, you can move on from "stress" to planning what you should do. Acceptance is a much better coping mechanism for unpleasant situations than stress.

- **Improves your relationship with yourself and, consequently, others.** Acceptance cultivates a kinder and more compassionate relationship with yourself, allowing you to treat yourself with understanding and forgiveness during difficult times. This, in turn, fosters deeper connections and healthier communication patterns, leading to more fulfilling relationships with others.

- **Reduces overthinking and rumination.** Overthinking is generally about the future, and rumination is about the past.

Overthinking involves excessive dwelling on a particular thought, problem, or situation. It often leads to analysis paralysis, where you become stuck in a cycle of analyzing every detail without reaching a decision. For example, you can't stop thinking about all the possible outcomes of going on a vacation with friends you just met. You're constantly weighing the pros and cons of going or not going without making progress.

Rumination specifically refers to repetitive thinking about distressing thoughts or feelings. You can't help but hit "Replay" on past unpleasant events. For example, you keep replaying a past argument in your mind, obsessing over what was said and how it made you feel, intensifying your negative emotions.

Acceptance reduces overthinking and rumination because it encourages you to unwaveringly recognize your thoughts and emotions—without judgment or resistance—instead of getting caught up in endless cycles of analyzing. Acceptance allows you to make peace with your thoughts and let them pass through your mind without becoming entangled in them.

Acceptance is not only highly beneficial in life, but I consider it the first step in any healing journey. I firmly believe that you must accept your current reality AS IS before you can move to change it.

Acceptance is a skill that takes time and practice to develop. It's not something you can just turn "On," especially if you've been avoiding or judging your thoughts and emotions for a long time. The good news is that with patience and practice, you CAN cultivate acceptance in your life. The following exercises will help you achieve this.

Exercise 5: Willing Hands

We experience emotions in our bodies. If you're finding it hard to accept a situation, this body-focused practice might help you cultivate a sense of openness within yourself.

Usually, when we're going through an unpleasant or difficult situation, we tend to curl our hands into tight fists. This time, do the opposite. That is, carefully open your hands and palms and relax your fingers.

If you continue to sense resistance, slowly open or stretch your hands, one finger at a time, until your hands are open wide and your fingers are wide apart (nearly tensing).

Next, slowly relax to a willing hands position (relaxed but open).

Exercise 6: Acknowledge, Allow, Accept

This exercise will help you practice acceptance by breaking it down into three simple steps.

Step 1: Acknowledge. Recognize your thoughts, feelings, and experiences without judgment or resistance. This involves acknowledging the reality of your internal and external experiences.

What do you want to acknowledge right now? What's your current reality?

Example: I'm grieving my dog, Charlie. No one understands how deep my pain is now that he's gone.

Step 2. Allow. Once you acknowledge your thoughts and feelings, allow them to be present. Let these thoughts and emotions exist without trying to distract yourself from them. Just sit with the feeling and allow it to pass naturally.

What do you want to allow right now?

Example: I'm allowing my feelings of grief, sadness, and loneliness to exist within me. I have a right to feel these emotions now that my dog is gone.

Step 3: Accept. Accept and make peace with your experiences.

Write down your acceptance statement.

Example: I accept the reality that my best friend is gone. I accept that I'm feeling incredibly sad and lonely right now. I accept that these emotions are part of my grieving process.

Exercise 7: Non-Judgmental People Watching

It's our nature to judge. We watch something on Netflix and judge it with a thumbs up or down. We hear music and judge it as amazing or "noise." We smell a new scent and judge it as "pleasant" or "unpleasant."

Judging goes against the practice of acceptance because it's a form of control or assessment over something that simply IS. Of course, we're allowed to have an opinion, but acceptance is not about forming an opinion about anything or anyone. It's accepting facts. It's acknowledging reality AS IS.

So, when it comes to unpleasant or difficult thoughts or emotions, try not to label or judge them as "good or "bad" or whether you should feel them or not. Don't analyze, evaluate, or judge. Just allow and accept. The following exercise is one of my favorite exercises to combat judgmental behavior.

1. **Select a public space** like a nearby park, coffee shop, or shopping mall where you can watch people come and go. Bring pen and paper with you. If possible, allow 30 minutes for this exercise.

2. **Sit where you can observe people** come and go. Ensure you have a clear view of different people doing different things, but not close enough that you can hear what they're saying.

3. Look around and notice someone. Pay attention to their gestures and facial expressions. Grab your pen and paper and write down your observations.

   Example: I notice a man walking ahead of a woman who seems to be his wife.

```
┌─────────────────────────────────────────────────────┐
│                                                       │
│                                                       │
│                                                       │
│                                                       │
└─────────────────────────────────────────────────────┘
```

4. Did your mind jump to any assumptions or judgments? If so, write them down. Note: DO NOT criticize yourself for having these thoughts.

Example: I don't know why, but I got annoyed and judged that the man was not considerate of his wife. I mean, why is he walking away and ahead of her?

```
┌─────────────────────────────────────────────────────┐
│                                                       │
│                                                       │
│                                                       │
│                                                       │
│                                                       │
│                                                       │
└─────────────────────────────────────────────────────┘
```

5. **Reflect.** Explore where your assumptions might have come from.

Example: I just never saw my dad "walk away" from my mom?

```
┌─────────────────────────────────────────────────────┐
│                                                       │
│                                                       │
│                                                       │
│                                                       │
│                                                       │
│                                                       │
└─────────────────────────────────────────────────────┘
```

6. **Challenge your assumptions.** WHAT ELSE could be true?

Example: Well, maybe the man and the woman are complete strangers to each other and not a couple at all.

```
┌─────────────────────────────────────────────────────┐
│                                                       │
│                                                       │
│                                                       │
│                                                       │
│                                                       │
└─────────────────────────────────────────────────────┘
```

┌───┐
│   │
│   │
│   │
└───┘

7. Move on to observe other people in different situations. Write down any immediate judgments you form about them, then immediately move on to challenging your assumptions. Continuously do this until your thinking slowly shifts to not forming automatic assumptions about others or until the 30 minutes is up.

8. After this exercise, shift your focus inward and practice self-compassion towards yourself for any judgments you may have made. Acknowledge that it's natural to have thoughts and opinions about others, but also recognize that you can choose NOT to do so.

9. Next, extend compassion to the people you observed. Recognize that everyone is navigating their own challenges and experiences and that you don't know their story or what they're going through that day.

10. Get up and leave the space where you did this exercise. And as you do, release any guilt or negative feelings regarding any judgments you may have made. Recognize that those judgments are simply passing thoughts. Allow them to come and go without getting caught up in them like clouds passing across the sky.

As you go about your day, make a conscious effort to practice nonjudgmental acceptance in your interactions with yourself and others. Notice when judgments arise and gently redirect your attention towards acceptance and compassion.

Chapter 4: Mindfulness (Present Moment Awareness)

Mindfulness is living in the present. It's existing in NOW. It involves paying attention to your thoughts, feelings, sensations, and surroundings–as they are happening–with openness and curiosity. Instead of getting caught up in worries about the past or the future, mindfulness helps you focus on the here and now. It's like shining a spotlight on your present existence and experience, whether you're eating, walking, or breathing, without letting your mind wander.

The practice of mindfulness is NOT NEW. It emerged as an integral part of Buddhist meditation practices around 2,500 years ago. It was initially developed to cultivate awareness, attention, and present-moment focus to *alleviate suffering* and *achieve enlightenment*.

Most people think mindfulness is just "woo-woo" or nonsense, but I think it makes perfect sense. If you just take a moment to sit and "be," you're giving yourself time; the time you need to mentally and emotionally distance yourself from pain, stress, and whatever negative feelings you're experiencing. (You alleviate your suffering.) And as you put that distance, you get to see things, situations, and people in a different light. Maybe, just maybe, the situation is not that bad after all. (You achieve enlightenment.)

~~Mindfulness is nonsense.~~

Mindfulness makes perfect sense.

What's the point of mindfulness in ACT? How does it help develop psychological flexibility? Have you ever had a moment where you did or said something, and the second you did it, you were suddenly filled with regret? That's the point of mindfulness: to prevent you from automatically reacting. It gives you the time, space, and opportunity to *think before you act*.

So, imagine mindfulness as a "mental pause button" you can click between "trigger" and "reaction." If you activate it, you give yourself time to focus on yourself, inwardly and outwardly, and to assess what your next step should be.

In real life, trigger+reaction happens fast. For example, if someone hurts you, you hurt back. And then they hurt you back, and then... you get the picture.

But if you're mindful, you can stop, reflect, and assess. At that exact stage of present-moment awareness, you're creating distance between yourself, your strong emotions, and any automatic reactions you want to make. Now, *choice* enters.

As that distance between trigger and knee-jerk reaction grows, alternatives come in. What else can you do? How can you make this situation better? And that, my friend, is *psychological flexibility*, the ability to withstand pain, stress, or the unexpected and shift perspective.

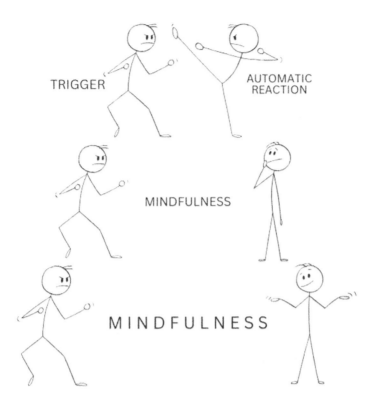

TRIGGER

AUTOMATIC
REACTION

MINDFULNESS

M I N D F U L N E S S

Important: The above image illustrates how mindfulness can help someone not react to a situation in a way that escalates it or makes it worse. This does not mean you're "okay" or "agree" with what happened. Also, your response after mindfulness can be varied. Depending on the situation or trigger, you might do the exact opposite of what you intended (e.g., sit down and calmly engage in a conversation vs. shouting angrily), or you might decide to walk away and return to the situation later. It all depends on the situation and what you want to achieve.

Let's consider another example: Max is stressed at work with deadlines up to his ears when his colleague, Bob, sends him an email on Friday at 4 PM asking him to review a project report due next Monday. Now, Max is already not a fan of Bob, so his knee-jerk, automatic reaction might be to send a nasty email back saying that he thinks it's crap that Bob is sending the email only now. He might even copy their boss to boot! Max might also pretend he didn't see the email and let everything fall on Bob's shoulders on Monday. Are any of these scenarios helpful in any way? Probably not.

Here's what practicing mindfulness might look like in this situation.

(1) **Take a break.** Max gets up, stretches his legs, grabs a cup of coffee or tea, and breathes deeply for a few minutes.

(2) **Accept reality as is.** Bob sent a last-minute email asking me to review a report I barely know anything about.

(3) **Accept your thoughts and emotions as is.** I'm angry and frustrated right now. That's okay. This is a normal reaction.

(4) **Evaluate the next steps.** What's the best way to handle this? What exactly do I want to happen in this situation? The reality is I don't have time for this report, and I want to set a boundary here.

(5) **Act accordingly and respond respectfully and tactfully (not angrily and accusatory).**

Dear Bob,

I just read your email. Normally, I would have no issues helping, but it's 4:15 PM, and I have no time to review this report because I also have a couple of mine to go over.

Kind regards and a happy weekend,
Max

As you can see, mindfulness prevented Max from worsening an already stressful situation. He said "No" and set a boundary, and by using simple and direct words that are more factual than emotional, he came across as completely reasonable and professional. Notice the lack of any "blaming" tone in the message as well.

Just like acceptance, mindfulness is a skill that needs to be developed. You may find that getting from "automatic reaction" to "best reaction" takes a long time. However, with constant mindfulness practice, you'll notice that your ability to alleviate your suffering and feel better becomes more efficient over time.

If you find yourself resisting mindfulness, you're not alone. Here are some of the most common roadblocks to mindfulness and what to do about them.

1. **Skepticism or doubt.** This is probably one of the strongest barriers to practicing mindfulness. You may not believe it will work, so you don't want to try it. But imagine this: say someone just met you and decided in that second they don't like you at all. Is that fair? Wouldn't it be better if that person tried to get to know you first? Think of mindfulness as a person you just met.

   What to do: Approach mindfulness with an open mind and a spirit of curiosity. Also, there are many ways to practice mindfulness, so experiment with different techniques to find what works best for you and explore without judgment.

2. **Busy lifestyles.** Everyone is busy. We're always in motion, always doing something, always trying to achieve and move up in life. We've even perfected the art of multi-tasking and dealing with unnecessary interactions. However, none of that erases the fact that we're also stressed and anxious. Wouldn't it be great to be unstressed and unanxious, even for a while?

What to do: Prioritize mindfulness by treating it like a sacred appointment with yourself. Schedule regular times for mindfulness practice, even just a few minutes daily. For example, set an alarm that goes off at the same time each day to remind yourself to take a break or meditate.

Also, look for opportunities to integrate mindfulness into your daily activities. For example, take 5 minutes to mindfully eat breakfast or spend 10 minutes after lunch to engage in mindful walking. Here's some funny advice I received from a mindfulness teacher a few years ago: If you have time to talk, you have time not to talk (and thus, be mindful).

3. **Constant digital distractions.** Focusing on the present moment when you're bombarded with 24/7 non-stop digital distractions is challenging.

What to do: Set digital boundaries by scheduling specific times for digital use and your mindfulness practice. For example, when practicing mindfulness, use features on your phone that limit distractions, such as its built-in Do Not Disturb modes. You can also use tools such as Cold Turkey (for desktops) or AppBlock (for mobile devices) to help you stay focused by blocking phone apps from sending you notifications.

4. **Stress and overwhelm.** Most people tell me they don't have enough time to "waste" on mindfulness because they're too stressed and overwhelmed with life. This is like saying, "I don't want to drink because I'm too thirsty."

What to do: Use mindfulness techniques, such as basic deep breathing or body scan meditation, to manage stress in the moment. You don't need to go "deep" with mindfulness. You don't need to overthink the practice. You can use it as you would take a warm bath or soothing massage to de-stress.

5. **Difficulty with concentration.** When I started my mindfulness practice, I found it hard to be still and concentrate for a few minutes. I found it hard to "not think." But then I had this nagging thought, "Hmmm, I thought I was in control of my mind. Why can't I command it to be still for just a few minutes?!" This thought bothered me because I felt like my mind had too much "noise" that I didn't want. I wanted to reach a stage where I could think clearly without noise or distractions. So, I kept being mindful until I reached this goal. And I know you can, too.

What to do: Be patient with yourself. Let go of any expectations and focus on one thing at a time mindfully rather than trying to juggle multiple thoughts simultaneously. When you practice mindfulness, let go of the word "multi-tasking" and embrace "single-tasking."

For example, if you're listening to music during your practice, just listen to the music and tune out anything else you might hear. If you hear a bird chirping outside, don't let your thoughts follow it. Don't mind wander. Just say or think "chirp," then return to the music. If you hear a passing car, say or think "car," then return to the music. Do this over and over. In time, you'll find it easier, almost automatic, to ignore external noise.

I like to think of mindfulness as "plugging in" or "recharging." Each time you practice it, imagine giving yourself that energy or juice to refresh your mind and well-being. Just like plugging in your phone to charge its battery, mindfulness allows you to replenish your mental and emotional energy, helping you feel more present, centered, and alive.

So, ready to meet and get to know mindfulness? Following are a few exercises to jumpstart your practice.

Exercise 8: Box Breathing or Square Breathing

Breathing is basic. We all know this; we all do this. But did you know that you might be breathing the wrong way?

Most people are shallow breathers, inhaling through the nose or mouth and then exhaling it out. We huff and puff, never letting air reach our diaphragms. So, the first thing you need to learn is how to properly breathe deeply. Why? The breath is important in cultivating mindfulness because it serves as an anchor to the present moment.

When you focus on your breath, you bring your attention to the sensations of breathing, which are always in the present moment. (You can't breathe in honor of yesterday or start breathing for tomorrow, right? Breathing is always about NOW.)

So, breathing deeply helps you become more aware of your thoughts, feelings, and physical sensations as they happen—without becoming entangled in them. Plus, the breath is always accessible, making it a convenient tool for practicing mindfulness anytime and anywhere. Let's start!

Step 1: Sit or lie down in a comfortable position. Make sure your spine is straight but not tense. You can place your hands on your lap or sides, whatever feels natural.

Step 2: Inhale slowly and deeply through your nose, counting to four as you breathe in. Feel your lungs expanding as you fill them with air. Try to breathe deeply into your belly rather than shallow breaths into your chest.

Step 3: Hold your breath for four counts. Keep your lungs filled with air, and your body relaxed as you hold your breath.

Step 4: Now, **exhale slowly through your mouth for four counts** as you release the air from your lungs. Feel the tension leaving your body with each exhale.

Step 5: After you've completed your exhale, **pause for another count of four**. This moment of pause allows you to reset and prepare for the next breath.

Step 6: Continue this box breathing pattern for several rounds, maintaining a steady rhythm and focusing on the sensation of your breath. You can do this for a few minutes or as long as you need to feel calm and centered.

Step 7: When you're done, take a moment to reflect. Pay attention to any changes in your body, mind, or emotions. After practicing this exercise, you may feel more relaxed, focused, or grounded.

Make box breathing a daily habit. Studies show that it provides quick stress and anxiety relief, lowers blood pressure, increases focus (not just during practice but throughout the day), and enhances the mind-body connection.[29] The more you practice, the easier it will become to tap into a sense of calm and balance whenever you need it.

Exercise 9: Mindful Walking in Nature

This exercise offers a multitude of benefits. In addition to training yourself to focus on the present, you interact with nature. Studies show that being outdoors can reduce stress levels, improve mood, and enhance overall well-being.[30] Additionally, walking in nature encourages physical activity. It's a win-win with this exercise.

Step 1: Find a peaceful outdoor location such as a park, forest trail, beach, or botanical garden. Aim for a place with minimal distractions and abundant natural beauty.

Step 2: Before you begin walking, take a moment to **set your intentions** for the practice. For example, write down or say to yourself, "I'm going to take a walk and just be with myself. I want to destress and enjoy my own company for a few minutes."

Step 3: Start by standing still in a comfortable position. Close your eyes if it feels comfortable, and **take a few deep breaths** to center yourself. Feel the sensation of your feet grounding into the earth beneath you.

Step 4: Open your eyes and begin to observe your surroundings. Don't choose what to focus on. Just let your eyes land on something and then try to observe it detachedly. For example, say your eyes land on a nearby bench; describe it. Notice its features (size, length, color, sturdiness, etc.), and try not to form any opinions about it (e.g., that bench looks dirty).

Step 5: Start walking slowly, deliberately paying attention to each step you take. Feel the earth beneath your feet with each stride. Maintain a relaxed and steady pace, allowing your movements to flow naturally.

Step 6: As you walk, **bring your attention to your breath**. Notice the rhythm of your inhales and exhales and how your body moves with each breath. Use your breath as an anchor to keep you grounded in the present moment.

Step 7: Continuously engage your senses as you walk. Notice the intricate details of the natural world around you—the patterns in tree bark, the shapes of clouds, the colors of flowers. Tune in to the sounds of nature, from the songs of birds to the rustling of leaves.

Step 8: You'll inevitably encounter various thoughts, emotions, and sensations during your walk. Practice observing them without judgment. If your mind starts to wander, gently bring your attention back to the present moment and the sensations of walking.

Step 9: At certain moments during your walk, **express gratitude**. You can say thanks for the beauty and abundance of nature surrounding you or simply appreciate your sturdy legs and feet for supporting your every step.

Step 10: When you're ready to conclude your walk, slow your pace and find a quiet spot to reflect. Take a few moments to think about your experience and acknowledge any insights or feelings you had during your walk. Offer yourself gratitude for taking the time to prioritize yourself.

Exercise 10: Grounding Using Your Five Senses

Mindfulness can also come to the rescue when you're in crisis. When we're in distress, it's easy for our thoughts to spiral out of control. It's like the past, present, and future collide inside you, and you can't stop overthinking or ruminating. One way to press STOP on that rollercoaster of stormy emotions is to bring yourself to the present moment using your five senses.

Step 1: Go to a quiet space where you can sit comfortably without any distractions. It could be indoors or outdoors, as long as you feel relaxed and at ease. There might be situations where you feel you can't just go and leave in the middle of a stressful situation, but you can. Say something like, "This isn't helping me/us. I need to take a break," or "This situation is stressing me. I need to regroup."

Step 2: Sit comfortably on a chair with your feet flat on the floor or cross-legged on the ground. Rest your hands on your lap or knees, whichever feels more comfortable.

Step 3: Take a few deep breaths or practice <u>Box Breathing</u>. Inhale deeply, and imagine any stress or tension moving away from you with each exhale.

Step 4: Now, focus on each of your five senses, one at a time:

- **Sight.** Look around and **notice five things you can see**. They could be objects in the room, colors, or patterns. Take a moment to observe each one without judgment, simply acknowledging its presence.

- **Hearing.** Close your eyes and **identify four things you can hear**. It could be the sound of traffic outside, birds chirping, water splashing, or the hum of appliances in the room. Tune in to each sound and let it wash over you.

- **Touch. Find three things you can touch or feel.** It could be the texture of the fabric beneath you, the coolness of the wall, or the smooth surface of an object nearby. Take a moment to fully experience the sensation of touch.

- **Smell.** Take a deep breath through your nose and **identify two things you can smell**. It could be the scent of flowers, food cooking nearby, or even the freshness of the air. Notice the aroma and how it affects your mood and state of mind.

- **Taste.** Finally, **focus on one thing you can taste**. It could be the lingering flavor of your last meal, the freshness of a mint, or simply the taste of your saliva. Allow yourself to fully experience this sensation, savoring it for a moment.

Step 5: After you've engaged all five senses, take a moment to **return to your breath**. Notice how your body feels now compared to when you started. Allow yourself to bask in the present moment, feeling grounded and centered.

Step 6: Before you end the exercise, take a moment to **reflect on one thing you're grateful for in this moment**. It could be that you're proud of yourself for taking the time to ground yourself to the present moment or something you noticed during the exercise.

Step 7: Take a deep breath and exhale as forcefully as possible. Stand up, stretch, or shake your arms and legs, whatever feels good for you. Next, take one confident step to join the rest of the world again.

Don't rush this exercise. If you need more time to ground yourself, then so be it. You can engage each of your senses again, one at a time.

Mindfulness of Emotions

We're always feeling something. There's not a moment when we're not experiencing an emotion. But when these emotions are the stressful, painful, and difficult kind, we might end up feeling depressed or that there's no hope.

One of the most helpful pieces of advice I received about emotions is this: **No single emotion lasts forever.**

Emotions are transient and tend to fluctuate over time. While some emotions may linger longer than others, eventually, they will fade or shift in intensity. This natural ebb and flow of emotions is a normal part of the human experience.

But WHY do we experience certain emotions? There's an internal process involved as to why we feel the way we do over something or someone.

Step 1: Trigger. This event, situation, or stimulus initiates the emotional response. It could be something external, like a comment from someone, or internal, like a memory.

Example: Sam walks down the street, and someone he knows walks past him without saying hello. This is the trigger.

Step 2: Filtering. Once the trigger occurs, your mind filters it through *your* beliefs, past experiences, and perceptions. This filtering process influences how you interpret and respond to the trigger.

Example: Sam interprets the other person's behavior through the filter of his past experiences. Maybe he's had issues with this person before, so Sam interprets their action as deliberate rudeness rather than a simple oversight.

Step 3: Subjective experience. This step involves your personal interpretation of the filtered information. It's where you assign meaning to the trigger based on your unique perspective, values, and understanding of the world.

Example: Sam feels hurt and slighted by their behavior. Based on his interpretation (filtering), Sam concludes that they don't like him or are intentionally ignoring him.

Step 4: Physiological response. Physiological changes, such as increased heart rate, sweating, or changes in breathing patterns, often accompany emotions. These physical sensations are part of the emotional experience.

Example: Sam's now annoyed by the whole event. His heart rate increases, and he's feeling flushed. This is his body reacting to the emotional distress of being, in his mind, deliberately ignored or snubbed.

Step 5: Behavioral response. Finally, your emotions lead to behavioral responses or actions. These can vary widely depending on the emotion, intensity, and who you are.

Example: Sam might, in the present moment, engage in specific behaviors or reactions (e.g., slamming a door, banging his fist on a table, etc.). In the future, when he sees the other person again, Sam might respond by avoiding eye contact or feeling angry and resentful toward them. This behavior is influenced by the emotions and interpretations he experienced in response to the trigger.

How does knowing this process help you? In the above example, the situation started with "someone not saying hello." Then, it quickly moved on to a personal interpretation of "deliberately being ignored" and feelings of resentment towards the ignorer.

But what does Sam know for sure? What's the FACT here? Someone passed by without saying hello. That's it.

The rest is Sam's *personal interpretation* of the situation. In reality, there could be plenty of reasons why Sam was ignored, none having anything to do with Sam. The other person might have eye problems and was not wearing his glasses that day and missed Sam, or they might be going through something and their mind was preoccupied with their problems.

In short, Sam could have stopped at Step 1: Trigger. He didn't have to go through steps 2-5 and feel bad about the whole thing.

When you are in crisis or distress, it helps to be mindful and aware of how you filter a trigger. It helps to remind yourself that how you see and interpret something may not accurately reflect the situation. When you do this, you prevent emotional and mental suffering.

So what do you do? When triggered, try to label or name the exact emotion you're feeling. This is because what you feel influences your thoughts and behavior. If you can address the emotion first, there's a good chance you can nip any potential negative thoughts and actions you might make.

Exercise 11: Name that Emotion

Did you know that naming or being able to identify a distressing emotion lessens its intensity, making you better able to handle a difficult situation?[31] The problem is that sometimes, it's hard to pinpoint exactly what we're feeling. For example, what are you feeling RIGHT NOW?

If you're unable to pick one, you might think it's because none of the above six emotions accurately reflect your feelings.

Maybe you're anxious? Confused? Excited? Jealous? Anything else? Whatever it is, understand that it's a totally valid emotion. However, you may not be aware that what you're experiencing is a *secondary emotion.*

Primary emotions (the six above) are our initial reactions to situations. Secondary emotions (or even tertiary ones) are our responses to our primary emotions. Here's an **Emotion Wheel**. Use it as you go through the following steps in this exercise.

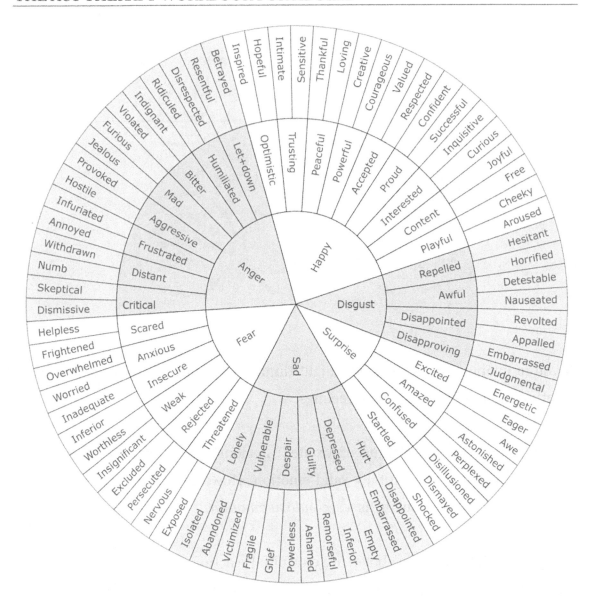

Step 1: Identify a trigger. Think about a recent event or situation that stirred up some strong emotions. It could be something positive, negative, or neutral. Take a moment to recall the details of the event.

Step 2: As you recall the situation, **pay attention to any physical sensations you're experiencing**. Is there any tightness, warmth, or discomfort in certain parts of your body? (Your body often provides clues about the emotions you're feeling.) If you're feeling discomfort, take a deep breath, and as you exhale, say, "Release." Keep on doing this until the negative bodily sensation lessens or evaporates.

Step 3: Look at the outer edges of the Emotion Wheel, and pick the word that describes your emotion RIGHT NOW.

Example: I feel disrespected.
I feel _____ .

Move to the inner circle and pick the word that describes your emotion even more.

Example: I feel disrespected -> humiliated.
I feel _____ -> _____ .

In the same section, look at the innermost circle of the wheel and write down the *primary emotion* you see.

Example: I feel disrespected -> humiliated -> anger.
I feel _____ -> _____->_____ .

Step 4: Now that you've narrowed down your primary emotion, **explore what this may mean**. Here's a table to help you.

Happiness	Sadness	Fear
something is important	*something is not right*	*there's potential danger*
Surprise	**Disgust**	**Anger**
a call to focus on new situations	*something is unhealthy for you*	*a need to protect something or fight a problem*

Step 5: Write down what it means to you to be able to name your primary emotion and understand what it means. Does it provide clarity and validation for what you're experiencing?

Reflect on why labeling emotions can help manage and understand your inner world. Write freely, and don't criticize or judge yourself. Let the words flow as you get to the root of your emotions.

Example: When Frank ignored me on the street, I felt disrespected and humiliated. I knew I was angry, but I didn't know that anger meant "wanting to protect something." So, what do I want to protect? My ego, I guess. And if my ego is so easily bruised... do I need to work on my self-esteem?

Step 6: After reflecting on your emotion, **consider how you want to express or process it**. This could involve journaling, talking to a friend or therapist, engaging in a creative activity, or simply allowing yourself to feel the emotion without judgment.

The better you can identify and define your emotions, the more effectively you can cope with them. Remember, you have every right to feel your emotions, but you don't necessarily need to act according to them.

Exercise 12: Mindful Body Scan of Emotions

This exercise aims to cultivate greater awareness and acceptance of the connection between physical sensations and emotional experiences. By systematically scanning your body and exploring sensations with a nonjudgmental attitude, you can learn to recognize and name your emotions more effectively.

Step 1: Choose a comfortable, quiet space to sit or lie down, free of distractions. Ensure you won't be interrupted during the exercise.

Step 2: Sit or lie down comfortably. **Close your eyes and take a few deep breaths** to center yourself.

Step 3: Direct your attention to your physical sensations. Notice the points of contact between your body and the supporting surface. Feel the weight of your body sinking into the chair or bed.

Step 4: Slowly shift your focus to different parts of your body, starting from your toes and gradually moving upward. Notice any sensations, tensions, or areas of discomfort as you scan each body part. Allow yourself to observe these sensations without judgment or the need to change them.

Step 5: As you scan each body part, **pay attention to any emotions or feelings that arise**. You might notice tension in your shoulders, a sense of warmth in your chest, or butterflies in your stomach. Take note of any emotional experiences without trying to analyze or interpret them.

Step 6: If you struggle to identify emotions, practice focusing on specific body parts. For example, if you feel tension in your jaw, gently direct your awareness to that area and notice any associated emotions, such as stress or frustration. You can ask yourself, "Why is my jaw so tense?" and then let the answer come to you.

Step 7: As you become aware of different emotions within your body, **practice accepting** them as valid and natural responses to your internal and external experiences. Allow yourself to feel whatever arises without resistance or judgment.

Step 8: Next, **breathe into your emotions**. With each breath, imagine sending gentle waves of relaxation and acceptance to the areas of your body where you're experiencing emotions. Use your breath to soothe and comfort yourself amid emotional discomfort.

Step 9: After scanning your entire body and exploring the associated emotions, **take a few moments to rest in this state of mindful awareness**. Notice how you feel physically, emotionally, and mentally after completing the exercise.

Step 10: When ready, **gently open your eyes and reflect** on your experience. Notice any insights or observations that arose during the body scan.

Tip: Doing this exercise often may reveal certain things. For example, say that you're often experiencing jaw tenseness. This might reveal that you're often angry. In this case, you might want to think about why you feel this way so often and what you can do to address it.

Chapter 5: Cognitive Defusion (a.k.a. Unhooking)

Here's a story from Elizabeth, or Lizzie, one of my readers.

A painter cousin of mine, James, came to visit one summer when I was about 12 years old. One day, he asked me to "strike a pose," and he'd make a quick sketch of me. I was quite shy, so I just sat there and smiled a little. After some time, James proclaimed, "Okay. I'm done!" My two older sisters sat beside me eagerly, and James turned his sketch around. It was my "pose," but it was a sketch of Miss Piggy.

My sisters burst into uncontrollable laughter. James was laughing, too. And for some reason, I started "laughing" as well. I guess I didn't want anyone to know just how devastated I was inside. I was embarrassed and angry; all I wanted to do was hide and cry. One afternoon. One sketch. And I was forever changed.

I started wearing very loose clothes. In my mind, I thought, "No one should ever think my clothes are too tight. What if someone comes over and pinches my "love handles?" I started to drastically eat less. I threw part of my packed lunch so my mom wouldn't know I wasn't eating all the food she packed for me. But then, most nights, I would binge eat because I was so hungry. Of course, I'd feel very guilty and disappointed with myself after that. Outwardly, I became even more shy and reserved. (I had only one decent friend in high school.) That feeling of being fat, of being Ms. Piggy, never left me.

As an adult, whenever I would get intimate with someone, the lights MUST be out. I had zero self-confidence in how I looked. During parties, I would demurely say no to food and just "nibble" even though I was dizzy with hunger. What if someone watched me eat and thought, "Wow, what a Miss Piggy." At work, I was so reserved that I barely voiced my ideas, meaning I often got passed for promotions or recognition. And then three things happened in the span of ONE week that changed everything—again. (But this time, for the better!)

First, my husband saw me in some new clothes and casually remarked, "Babe, that dress is too big for you." Second, I was at the gym, and as I got out of the shower with nothing but a towel around me, a gym employee said, "Hey, Lizzie, you're... a lot smaller than I thought you were! Why do you always wear baggy clothes out there?" These instances baffled me. For the first time, I thought, "Am I not as "big" as I think I am?"

Lastly, I ran into a friend I hadn't seen in years. She just got divorced and came back to the neighborhood. We scheduled to meet for coffee a week later, and as we caught up on each other's lives, she shared that she was seeing an ACT therapist to help her through the divorce. "ACT? What's that?" She told me about it, and I was so intrigued that I started researching on my own after that conversation.

I learned many life-changing things with ACT, but particularly enlightening was "cognitive fusion." I realized this is what I've been doing since I was 12.

I was "fused" to the thought that I was Miss Piggy. Actually, to be more accurate, I was fused to the thought that others perceived me as Miss Piggy, and all my actions have followed that thought since then. I felt a lot of sadness and regret as I learned about this concept. I came to terms with the fact that I heaped a lot of unnecessary shame on myself and did *a lot of "hiding." I also regretted my resulting eating habits, which I believe harmed my health. (I'm taking steps to remedy that now.)*

I continue to do self-guided ACT at home, practicing cognitive defusion to unglue myself from my "Miss Piggy" belief. I'm not there yet, but I'm hopeful.

ACT proposes that individuals often become fused or entangled with their thoughts. This "fusion" can lead to mental, physical, and emotional distress when individuals believe and behave upon these thoughts without considering their accuracy or helpfulness.

For example, suppose Lizzie hadn't fused to the thought that people saw her as Miss Piggy. In that case, it's highly possible that she would not have drastically changed her eating habits, and her self-esteem would not have plummeted.

Here's another example: suppose you have social anxiety and believe, "If I make a mistake while speaking in public, everyone will think I'm stupid." This thought might become fused with your sense of self, leading you to avoid social situations altogether. Even if you've had successful presentations in the past, you ignore these facts because your belief is so strong and deeply ingrained. Your assumption that "public speaking mistake = stupidity" constantly influences your emotions and behavior, perpetuating your anxiety about public speaking.

So, how do you unglue or unhook yourself from unhelpful thoughts? You practice cognitive **de**fusion.

Cognitive defusion or mental defusion is about changing the way you relate to your thoughts. Think of your mind as a busy street, with thoughts rushing like cars. Cognitive defusion is like stepping onto the sidewalk and watching cars (i.e., your thoughts) come and go rather than getting caught up in the traffic. By creating distance between yourself and your thoughts, you remove their ability to control or dictate your emotions and actions.

In short, cognitive defusion teaches you that "Thoughts" does not equal "Self." So, to remove or lessen the power or control of "Thoughts," you must learn to put distance between them and the "Self." Why? **Although you are not your thoughts, you can become them**. (What you think, you become.) Cognitive defusion is all about preventing you from becoming your negative thoughts.

"Becoming that person" in ACT is often referred to as the "conceptualized self" or "concretized self."

The **conceptualized self** is how you see yourself based on your thoughts and ideas about who you are. It's like a mental picture of yourself that you create by thinking about your qualities, roles, and how you fit into the world. For example, you might see yourself as a "successful business owner," a "caring parent," or a "good friend" because of how you think about your experiences and what's important to you.

Characteristics: How you think and evaluate yourself shapes your conceptualized self. It includes your personality, accomplishments, and how you see yourself in relationships and society.

Function: Your conceptualized self helps you make sense of your life and guides how you behave and make choices. It's like a mental map that helps you understand who you are and how you fit into the world around you.

The **concretized self** is like being trapped in a rigid idea of who you are. It happens when you get stuck on certain labels or stories about yourself and can't see beyond them. For example, if you've always seen yourself as a "successful professional," you might find it difficult to cope if you face setbacks in your career.

Characteristics: The concretized self feels unchanging and unyielding. You might need to defend this identity, even if it doesn't feel right anymore. It's like being stuck in one version of yourself.

Function: While having a fixed identity can feel secure, it can also hold you back from growing and being true to yourself. It might make you feel stuck or unhappy when life throws you curveballs.

Picture this: Someone feels really sad and lonely. They start to think of themselves as depressed, and their actions follow suit. They withdraw from family and friends and hardly go out anymore. As time goes on, they become deeply fused to this idea that they're not just feeling depressed; they're suffering from depression. The *thought* of being depressed (conceptualized self) becomes a solid part of who they are (concretized self).

So, no, you are not your negative or unhelpful thoughts, but you can become them. And even if you've already started down that path, remember, you can break free and "unhook" yourself from them by practicing cognitive defusion techniques.

Exercise 13: Thought Labeling

This exercise is designed to help you manage unhelpful thoughts. By learning to label your thoughts, you can create distance and reduce their impact on your mood and behavior.

1. **Find a quiet and comfortable space** where you can sit undisturbed for a few minutes. Take a few deep breaths to **center yourself** and bring your attention to the present moment.

2. Tune into your body and **notice any physical sensations**, such as tension, rapid heartbeat, or shallow breathing. Acknowledge these sensations without judgment or criticism.

3. **Write down your thoughts.** Grab pen and paper and identify the thought or thoughts you want to address. Write down one thought per piece of paper. These might include worries about your future, negative thoughts about yourself, doubts about your performance at work, etc. Important: Write down your thoughts without getting entangled in them. Remember, they are just thoughts, not necessarily facts or truths.

   Example: I'm fat and ugly. No one finds me lovable.

   Thought, belief, or assumption #1:

   Thought, belief, or assumption #2:

```
┌─────────────────────────────────────────────────────────┐
│                                                           │
│                                                           │
│                                                           │
│                                                           │
│                                                           │
└─────────────────────────────────────────────────────────┘
```

```
┌─────────────────────────────────────────────────────────┐
│ Thought, belief, or assumption #3:                        │
│                                                           │
│                                                           │
│                                                           │
│                                                           │
│                                                           │
│                                                           │
│                                                           │
└─────────────────────────────────────────────────────────┘
```

4. Next, **label your thoughts**. As you identify your thoughts, practice labeling them **in a neutral and non-judgmental** way. Use simple and descriptive labels to identify the content of your thoughts without getting caught up in their emotional impact. (**Tip**: Remove the word "I" in your labeling.)

Example:
Thought: I'm fat and ugly.
Thought label: negative body image

```
┌─────────────────────────────────────────────────────────┐
│ Thought, belief, or assumption #1:                        │
│ Thought label #1:                                         │
│                                                           │
│                                                           │
│                                                           │
│                                                           │
│                                                           │
│                                                           │
└─────────────────────────────────────────────────────────┘
```

```
┌─────────────────────────────────────────────────────────┐
│ Thought, belief, or assumption #2:                        │
│ Though label #2:                                          │
│                                                           │
│                                                           │
└─────────────────────────────────────────────────────────┘
```

```



```

Thought, belief, or assumption #3:
Though label #3:

5. **Practice acceptance.** After labeling a thought, take a moment to observe it without judgment. For example, say, "This is a thought I'm having today."

6. **Create distance between yourself and each labeled thought.** After practicing acceptance of your thought, stand up and take a physical step back from the thought. Observe the written thought from a distance, like an impartial observer. Remind yourself that The Thought is just a passing mental event, not necessarily a reflection of reality.

7. After labeling and creating distance, **gently let the thought go**. Sit back down, crumple the piece of paper with the thought, and throw it away. As you do so, imagine the thought drifting away like a leaf on a stream or a cloud in the sky.

8. Continue practicing thought labeling for several minutes, allowing yourself to observe and label each thought that arises. If your mind starts to wander

or you become distracted, gently bring your focus back to the present moment and resume the exercise.

9. When you're done, take a few moments to ground yourself in the present moment by focusing on your breath or connecting with your senses.

Exercise 14: Closing Thought Tabs

Here's another exercise designed to help you manage unhelpful thoughts. However, unlike the previous one (Thought Labeling), this exercise asks you to "close" negative thought patterns like closing browser tabs on a computer.

1. **Find a quiet and comfortable space** where you can sit undisturbed for a few minutes. **Close your eyes** and take a few deep breaths to **center yourself** and bring your attention to the present moment.

2. Tune into your body and **notice any physical sensations**, such as tension, rapid heartbeat, or shallow breathing. Acknowledge these sensations without judgment or criticism.

3. **Identify your thoughts.** Imagine your mind as a browser with multiple tabs open. Select a mental tab and identify any thoughts, beliefs, or assumptions that have persisted in your life and may have had a negative or unhelpful impact.

   Example: I always mess things up.

Select another mental tab and identify any thoughts, beliefs, or assumptions that may have a negative or unhelpful impact.

Example: No one likes me.

If you want to, select another mental tab and identify any thoughts, beliefs, or assumptions that may have a negative or unhelpful impact.

Example: Everyone's always conspiring against me!

4. **Close your mental tabs.** Visualize these thought tabs cluttering your mental space. So, mentally close each negative thought tab in your mind's browser one by one. Visualize clicking on the "X" button and watching the tab disappear. As you close each tab, say to yourself, "This is just a thought. I am choosing to close the doors on this thought now."

5. **Replace closed thought tabs with positive affirmations.** After closing each negative thought tab, replace it with a positive affirmation or self-affirming statement.

   Example:
   Closed thought tab: I always mess things up.
   Positive affirmation: I also do good, maybe even great, things. And I can learn from any mistakes I make.

6. **Practice self-compassion.** Throughout this exercise, practice self-compassion and kindness toward yourself. Recognize that negative thoughts are a normal part of being human, and it's okay to have them—and to let them go. Offer comfort and reassurance to yourself as you work through the process of closing thought tabs.

7. **Check your mental browser.** Take a moment to check in with your mental browser and notice if any new negative thought tabs have opened. If you notice any new tabs, repeat the process of closing them and replacing them with positive affirmations.

8. When you're done with this exercise, **slowly open your eyes and take a few moments to ground yourself in the present moment** by focusing on your breath or connecting with your senses.

Exercise 15: Externalizing Thoughts

This exercise is designed to help you manage negative, difficult, or unhelpful thoughts or emotions by externalizing and reframing them. By separating yourself from your thoughts and viewing them from a different perspective, you can reduce their intensity and regain control.

Note: This exercise uses "feelings of loneliness" as an example. Feel free to replace it with whatever thought, assumption, or belief you may be experiencing.

1. **Find a quiet and comfortable space** where you can sit undisturbed for a few minutes. Take a few deep breaths to **center yourself** and bring your attention to the present moment.

2. **Tune into your emotions** and notice any feelings of loneliness that you're experiencing. Acknowledge and validate these feelings without judgment or self-criticism. For example, say to yourself, "I'm feeling alone right now. I feel like there's not a single person in the world who cares for me."

3. **Externalize your thoughts** by imagining them as separate entities outside of yourself. You can name them or visualize them as characters in a story. For example, if you're thinking, "I'll always be alone," you might imagine it as a character named "Lonely Voice."

4. With each externalized thought, **create distance** by mentally placing it outside yourself, like setting it down on a table or putting it in a box. Visualize yourself stepping back from the thought and observing them from a distance, as if you were watching a scene in a movie.

5. **Initiate dialogue** with your externalized thought, addressing it directly as if it were a separate being. For example, ask "Lonely Voice" questions like, "Why are you here?" or "What do you want?" to explore the underlying motivations or beliefs behind your lonely thoughts. For instance, asking Lonely Voice, "Why are you here?" may reveal that you long to talk to someone right now or you're missing a specific person.

6. Once you've externalized your lonely thoughts, **challenge any associated negative thinking patterns** by reframing the situation more rationally and compassionately.

Example:
Lonely Voice: I feel lonely because no one likes me enough to get to know me.

Reframed Perspective: I feel lonely now, but this feeling doesn't define my worth. It's possible that others may not have had the chance to know me yet, and there are people out there who will appreciate and value me for who I am.

[ ]

7. **Practice self-compassion.** Throughout this exercise, practice self-compassion and kindness toward yourself. Remind yourself that loneliness is a common human experience. It doesn't define your whole worth or value, and it's a feeling that doesn't have to be permanent.

8. When you finish this exercise, **take a few moments to ground yourself in the present momen**t by focusing on your breath or connecting with your senses. Notice any shifts in your emotional state and any sense of relief or empowerment from externalizing your thoughts.

Exercise 16: The Defusion Wheel

The Defusion Wheel is a tool to help you gain psychological distance between unhelpful or negative thoughts and yourself. Simply spin the wheel and try out the technique it lands on. Some tasks will be short and easy to do, while others will require effort and time. Now, take a deep breath, keep an open mind, and spin that wheel!

1. **Sing or repeat**. This technique calls on you to sing or repeat the unhelpful thought playfully or exaggeratedly, which can help reduce its emotional impact. For example, if you're thinking, "I'm not good enough," you could sing it to the tune of the "Happy Birthday" song, a nursery rhyme, etc. You can also repeat the thought for about 60 seconds in a silly voice. (Think Minions or Chipmunks.)

2. **Literalize.** Treat thoughts literally (i.e., thinking of them as words, symbols, cartoon characters, etc.) rather than allowing them to have their usual emotional impact on you. This helps you see the thought as just words rather than a reflection of reality.

Example:

Unhelpful Thought: "I'm drowning in paperwork!"

Literalizing: Imagine drowning in paperwork, but picture a funny image instead of feeling overwhelmed. You might visualize yourself swimming through a sea of different colored sheets of paper. And then a colleague throws you a life ring from the elevator, the cafeteria, or... it doesn't matter, it's your funny visual, so your colleague (or someone else) can throw it from anywhere!

The point is, by literalizing the thought "I'm drowning in paperwork," you realize that it's just a metaphorical expression and that it's not humanly possible to "drown" in "paperwork." As such, any negative or difficult emotion resulting from the thought should lessen or disappear.

3. **Thank your mind.** Acknowledge your mind's efforts to protect you, even if its methods are sometimes unhelpful. For example, if you're experiencing anxious thoughts, you might thank your mind for trying to keep you safe but gently remind yourself that you're okay in this moment. This is acknowledging the thought without attaching significance to it.

4. **Visualize.** Imagine unhelpful thoughts and beliefs as objects passing by like clouds floating in the sky, cars coming and going on the highway, leaves floating down a river, a favorite slice of cake that, for some reason, you cannot fathom, always disappears way too fast when put in front of you.

5. **Mind questioning.** Instead of dismissing a thought, take a more curious approach towards it. The beauty of this technique is that you can picture your mind as an organ in your body that generates thoughts. This takes you further away from the Thoughts=Self conviction. Here are some sample questions you can ask your mind.

   - *Dear mind, what are you saying? What are you trying to tell me?*
   - *Hmmm, is this thought helpful or useful in any way? Why? Why not?*
   - *Dear mind, where did this thought come from? Is it based on a past experience? Someone said to me? A fear about the future?*
   - *Dear mind, what evidence supports this thought I'm having? What evidence contradicts it?*

6. **Personalize.** Give your unhelpful thought a funny or ridiculous name to reduce its power over you. For example, if you're thinking, "I'll never succeed," you could call it the "Negative Nancy" thought, which helps create distance and lightens the mood.

7. **Write it down.** Take the unhelpful thought and write it down on a piece of paper or in a journal. Seeing it written can help you detach from it and recognize it as just a passing thought rather than an absolute truth.

8. **Let it go.** Practice letting the unhelpful thought pass by without giving it any further attention or importance. For example:

- Imagine the thought as a feather and blow it away.
- Imagine the thought as a speck on your shirt and flick it away.
- Light a match or candle, imagine the flame representing your thought, and blow it out.

Perception vs. Reality

In the realm of cognitive defusion, one of the key concepts to explore is the distinction between perception and reality.

Perception is how we see and understand the world around us. Our past experiences, beliefs, and biases influence it. Now, while our perceptions may feel real to us, they are not always an accurate reflection of reality. (Unfortunately, our minds can sometimes twist things based on how we see them.)

Cognitive defusion involves challenging the validity and truthfulness of our perceptions. It encourages us to question the stories we tell ourselves and examine whether they align with objective reality or are merely products of our subjective interpretation.

For example, suppose you receive your boss's feedback on a work project. When you open the document, there are several comments, questions, and a hefty dose of corrections. Your initial perception might be that you are a failure and incapable of performing your job well. This perception could trigger feelings of inadequacy, self-doubt, and maybe even anxiety, leading you to avoid similar projects in the future.

Here's a reality check: Receiving constructive criticism is normal for professional growth and development. It doesn't necessarily mean that you're incompetent. For all you know, your boss might have been impressed by your work since the project was a really big and difficult one. By defusing the thought that you are inherently flawed, you can reframe the situation more accurately and constructively.

So, perception and reality are not always synonymous. The following exercises will help you distinguish between the two.

Exercise 17: I Am...

This exercise aims to help you acknowledge and appreciate the factual aspects of yourself, fostering self-awareness and self-acceptance. By focusing on objective truths rather than subjective judgments, you can cultivate a deeper understanding of your identity and strengths.

1. **Find a comfortable and quiet space** where you can reflect without distractions. Bring pen and paper and create a calming atmosphere by dimming the lights, playing soft music, or lighting a candle.

2. Sit in a relaxed position, allowing your body to unwind and your mind to **focus on the present moment**. Take a few deep breaths to center yourself and release any tension.

3. Start to **reflect on facts about yourself**. Starting each sentence with "I Am," write down factual statements that describe various aspects of yourself, such as your physical appearance, personality traits, skills, talents, accomplishments, and roles.

Provide Details: Include specific details or examples to support each statement. Instead of generalizing, provide concrete evidence or anecdotes that illustrate the truth of each fact. This adds depth and authenticity to your self-reflection. For example, don't just write down, "I am empathetic," state, "I am empathetic. I often listen carefully to people and try to understand their perspectives."

Avoid Value Judgments: Refrain from attaching value judgments or interpretations to the facts you list. Focus on describing your true self without assigning labels or evaluating their significance.

Examples:
I am fit. My BMI is 20, I run half-marathons, and strength train twice weekly.
I am punctual. I can't remember the last time I was late for anything.

I am _____

I am _____

I am _____

I am _____

I am _____

I am _____

I am _____

I am _____

I am _____

I am _____

4. **Practice self-acceptance** by embracing each fact as an integral part of who you are. Recognize that your worth is not determined by external standards or comparisons to others.

5. Take a moment to **review the list** of facts you've written about yourself. Notice any patterns or themes that emerge, highlighting recurring qualities or aspects of your identity. For example, suppose you notice a few facts related to fitness. In that case, it shows that this is a significant area of your life you may be unaware of.

6. **Internalize your truths.** Go over the facts you've identified, allowing them to sink in and integrate into your self-concept. Remind yourself of these truths whenever self-doubt or insecurity arises.

7. **Express gratitude** for the unique qualities and attributes that make you who you are. Appreciate the diversity of experiences and perspectives that shape your identity, fostering a sense of gratitude for your journey.

8. **Be kind and compassionate towards yourself** as you reflect on your list of facts. Offer yourself encouragement and support, acknowledging the value and worth inherent in your identity.

9. **Conclude the exercise with positive affirmations.** Reinforce your self-worth and confidence by saying affirmations such as "I am worthy," "I am enough," or "I am proud of who I am."

Exercise 18: Socratic Questioning

Sometimes, it's not enough to distance ourselves from negative thoughts about ourselves. We need to challenge it actively!

Socratic questioning is a technique to challenge and reframe negative or irrational thoughts. It involves asking probing questions to help you examine the evidence and validity of your thoughts or perceptions about yourself.

Although traditionally associated with CBT, Socratic questioning also applies in ACT because it promotes mindfulness and cognitive defusion, encouraging you to observe your thoughts with curiosity and openness.

Note: This exercise uses the negative thought "not good enough in a relationship" as an example. Feel free to replace it with whatever thought, assumption, or belief you may be experiencing.

1. **Identify a negative belief** or thought you have about yourself.

   Example: I'm not good enough for my partner.

2. **Explore the evidence.** Examine the evidence that supports this belief. Ask yourself what specific experiences or thoughts have contributed to this belief.

   - **The Past.** Are there any specific situations or events in the past that have led you to believe you're not good enough for your partner? In short, what do you think caused this belief?

     Example: I've had many failed relationships before.

(empty box)

- **The Present.** What evidence do you have that supports the belief that you're not good enough for your partner? For example, has your partner ever told you that you're not good enough for them, that you're "less" in any way, etc.

Example: No, not really. I just feel this.

(empty box)

---

3. **Think about the impact.**

- How is your negative thought affecting your daily life and overall well-being?

Example: I'm so anxious about my partner leaving that I feel unauthentic in this relationship. I feel like I just go along with what they want and don't really know what I want.

(empty box)

- Do you think your negative thoughts affect your partner and how they view your relationship?

Example: I'm not sure. Maybe they are tired of me assuming the worst all the time in our relationship?

4. **Consider alternative perspectives.** Encourage yourself to consider alternative perspectives that contradict your negative beliefs.

- What evidence do you have that *contradicts* the belief that you're not good enough for your partner? For example, can you think of times when your partner has expressed appreciation or affection towards you?

Example: Actually, my partner is very affectionate. We go out on date nights, and we cuddle a lot.

- List the positive qualities or strengths that you bring to the relationship.

Example: I'm loyal and loving. I'm empathic and very supportive.

5. **Reframe your negative thoughts** into a more balanced and realistic perspective based on your exploration and analysis.

- Instead of thinking, "I'm not good enough for my partner," reframe the belief to "I deserve love and respect in my relationship."
- Focus on affirming your worthiness and value as an individual, independent of external validation from your partner.

6. **Practice self-compassion.** Finish this exercise by extending self-compassion and kindness towards yourself. Remind yourself that it's normal to have insecurities and doubts, but you can challenge and overcome them.

Chapter 6: Self as Context

"Self as context" refers to that part of you that remains constant and unchanged regardless of the thoughts, feelings, sensations, or experiences you may have. It's like the background against which your thoughts and experiences occur.

For example, think of yourself as a vast sky and your thoughts and experiences as passing clouds. No matter how many clouds come and go, the sky remains unchanged, right? Similarly, no matter your thoughts or feelings, the essence of who you are remains constant.

Understanding "self as context" helps you gain perspective on your thoughts and experiences by encouraging you to see yourself as an *observer* of your thoughts rather than being defined by them.

As previously discussed, individuals experiencing mental and emotional distress or who feel like they are living unhappy lives have often reached a stage where they have *fused* a negative thought or belief into their sense of self to the point that they cannot see anything else.

Do you remember Lizzie? Seeing herself sketched as "Miss Piggy" changed her subsequent thoughts, emotions, and behavior. In her mind, Miss Piggy wasn't just a character; Lizzie was Miss Piggy, and Miss Piggy was Lizzie.

This fusion led Lizzie to overlook all the other aspects of her identity and worth. She forgot about her roles as a daughter, friend, colleague, and wife. She lost sight of her great qualities like loyalty, hard work, and reliability. The negative mental associations she carried about herself overshadowed all these positive attributes.

So, in a state of unhappiness, a negative thought, let's call it "X," can dominate your entire identity. However, by applying the "self as context" concept, you can transition into the role of an observer. You are not "X." You are an observer of "X."

By adopting the role of the observer, you become less reactive to challenging thoughts and emotions. Also, remember that as an *observer*, you can be as distant or close to what you're noticing, observing, or witnessing. This means you can shift from a single focus (a single negative thought) to the big picture (your life and everything in it.)

For example, imagine your life like a big stage show you're watching. There are lots of things happening on stage—your thoughts, feelings, and all the stuff you can see, hear, touch, taste, and smell. But here's the cool part: a part of you steps back, sits in the crowd, and watches the show. (You are now the observer or the "Observing Self.")

Sometimes, you might want to focus the stage spotlight on just one thing, like what you do when you focus on your breathing during a mindfulness exercise. Other times, you may want to zoom out and watch multiple things simultaneously. Either way, by being an observer and watching yourself in different situations, you prevent getting too caught up in your own story.

Exercise 19: Notice-Observe-Watch (NOW)

This mindfulness practice is designed to cultivate present-moment awareness and deepen your understanding of your thoughts, emotions, and sensations—as an observer.

Step 1: Notice.

1. **Find a comfortable and quiet space** to sit or lie down, free of distractions. Close your eyes if it feels comfortable, or maintain a soft gaze.

2. Take a few deep breaths to **center yourself** and bring your attention to the present moment. Notice the sensation of the breath as it enters and leaves your body without trying to control or change it.

3. Slowly **expand your awareness** to include your thoughts, emotions, bodily sensations, and environment. Notice whatever arises in your experience without judgment or attachment.

4. **As you become aware of different thoughts, emotions, and sensations, gently label them in your mind.** For example, "I notice tension in my shoulders," "I observe feelings of anxiety," or "I'm aware of sounds in the room."

5. **Approach your experience with curiosity and openness**, as if observing it from a distance. Notice any tendencies to get caught up in particular thoughts or emotions, and gently guide your attention back to the present moment.

Step 2: Observe.

1. **Shift your focus to observing your thoughts, emotions, and sensations.** Notice their characteristics, intensity, and patterns without trying to change or analyze them. For example, you might observe, "This tension on my shoulders. I'm observing that I feel it more on my left shoulder than on my right."

2. **Practice non-attachment.** Allow your thoughts and emotions to come and go like clouds passing through the sky. Avoid getting entangled in the content of your experience or trying to suppress or avoid uncomfortable sensations. For example, say, "I acknowledge this discomfort on my left shoulder."

3. **Notice resistance.** If you encounter resistance or discomfort during this process, acknowledge it with kindness and curiosity. Explore any

underlying thoughts or beliefs contributing to your resistance without judgment. For example, you might say, "I seem unable to move on from the tension I feel on my left shoulder. I wonder why this is really bothering me. Could I've had this discomfort before and just not realized it?"

4. **Practice accepting** whatever arises in your experience, whether pleasant or unpleasant. Embrace the full spectrum of the human experience with compassion.

Step 3: Watch.

1. **Shift to the observer mindset.** Imagine yourself stepping back and assuming the role of the impartial observer of your inner and outer experience. Adopt a detached perspective, as if you were watching a movie of your life unfolding.

2. **Witness your experience.** Watch your thoughts, emotions, and sensations as they arise and pass away in the present moment. Notice the impermanent nature of your experience and the inherent fluidity of your inner world.

3. **Practice detached presence.** Remain anchored in the present moment without getting caught up in the storyline of your thoughts or emotions. If your mind wanders, gently guide your focus back to the present moment. Imagine yourself as a mountain that remains steadfast amidst shifting weather patterns.

4. **Express gratitude.** Conclude the exercise by expressing gratitude for your ability to observe and witness your experience with mindfulness and presence.

Exercise 20: The Participant vs. The Observer

This exercise helps you understand the difference between experiencing thoughts and feelings as a participant versus observing them as an impartial observer. Why is this important?

When you're caught up in the role of a participant, it's easy to become overwhelmed by your thoughts and feelings, leading to impulsive reactions and increased distress.

By cultivating the ability to step back and observe your inner experience from a place of detachment, you create space for reflection and insight. This, in turn, influences your behavior. Changing how you perceive your thoughts, feelings, and sensations can change how you act moving forward.

Note: The exercise below uses "chronic pain" as an example. Please feel free to modify it to fit your specific needs.

Important: As with all exercises mentioned in this book, the purpose of this exercise is NOT to deny pain or suffering in life. Acceptance teaches us that these are part of the human experience. This exercise aims to help decrease pain by helping you see it from a different angle.

1. **Find a quiet and comfortable space** to sit or lie down, free of distractions. Take a few deep breaths to center yourself and bring your focus to the present moment.

2. Reflect on the concept of being a participant versus an observer. Being a participant means actively engaging with your thoughts and feelings while being an observer means stepping back and noticing them without judgment.

3. **Identify chronic pain sensations.** Take a moment to tune into your body and notice any sensations of chronic pain that you're experiencing. Pay attention to the pain's location, intensity, and characteristics (e.g., sharp, throbbing, etc.). Allow yourself to fully acknowledge these sensations without trying to change them.

    Example: I have chronic headaches. I feel heaviness on my head and throbbing pain in the front of my head.

4. **Enter the participant mode.** Visualize yourself fully immersed in the experience of chronic pain. Allow yourself to feel the sensations as if actively participating in them. **Warning**: Doing this may exacerbate the pain. If you feel extreme discomfort, please discontinue.

    As you focus on being a participant, notice any thoughts or emotions that arise in response to the pain.

    Example: My headache is getting worse. I feel sad and depressed. I'm crying now.

Acknowledge your emotions and experience with kindness and understanding. Say to yourself, "It's okay to feel sad and overwhelmed right now. I'm here for myself. I will get through this challenging moment."

5. **Shift to observer mode.** Change your perspective to that of an impartial observer.

- Take a deep breath, and as you exhale, imagine yourself stepping back from pain sensations and observing them from a distance. Watch your pain as if you're watching something on a screen. Say to yourself, "I am not "pain." I am experiencing pain."
- Observe any accompanying sensations, such as tension, heat, or discomfort, with a sense of openness and curiosity.
- Acknowledge any thoughts or emotions that arise in response to the pain without judgment, allowing them to come and go like passing clouds in the sky.
- Remind yourself that it's okay to feel pain and that you can handle it with mindfulness and compassion.

Tip: Are you experiencing resistance shifting to observer mode? That's natural. Practice Willing Hands to open yourself up to this part of the exercise.

If you prefer a more "active" way of being an observer, great! Research shows that gentle, mindful movement exercises such as yoga, tai chi, or qigong help alleviate pain.[32,33,34,35] For example, when experiencing pain, try yoga, and with each gentle, mindful, and purposeful move, observe how your pain is reacting to your breath and movements.

6. Ask yourself the following **reflective questions**:

   - How did your level of involvement influence your pain?
   - As a participant, did your pain worsen?
   - As an observer, did your pain decrease?

7. Slowly bring your awareness back to the present moment. When ready, return to your day with a renewed sense of mindfulness and self-awareness in managing chronic pain.

8. **Integration.** Consider how you can apply this concept daily with chronic pain. Consider how adopting an observer mindset could help you respond more effectively to pain flare-ups and manage your emotional reactions.

9. **Commit to practicing this exercise regularly**, especially during moments of heightened pain or discomfort. The more you cultivate the ability to observe your chronic pain with curiosity and compassion, the greater your sense of control and resilience will become.

10. If you feel like it, **journal about your experience** with chronic pain and this exercise. Write down insights, observations, challenges, or areas for further exploration.

This exercise is NOT easy. Express gratitude to yourself for being open to exploring your experience with chronic pain in a new way.

Chapter 7: Values Clarification

What are your values? What do you want your life to be about? What kinds of qualities do you want to develop in yourself? What kind of person do you want to be in your relationships?

Your values are the things you consider most important in your life. They're like guiding principles that help you decide what's right or wrong and what you want to focus on or prioritize.

Your values might include honesty, kindness, family, friendship, success, or adventure. They're like a compass that helps you navigate life, making choices and decisions that align with what matters most to you.

Living a values-based life is at the core of ACT. It's one of the main aspects that make this therapy different from all other therapies. ACT emphasizes that if you clarify your values and live according to them, you live authentically. This, in turn, leads to happiness in life.

Values → Authenticity → Happiness

Unfortunately, not many of us live life according to our values. As a child, we live according to the values of our parents. When we go out into the world, we live life according to the values dictated by society. In relationships, we often prioritize our partners' or peers' expectations and desires over our values. This can lead to feelings of disconnection from our authentic selves and dissatisfaction and unhappiness with our lives.

ACT helps alleviate any mental, physical, or emotional suffering you may be experiencing by teaching you how to align your behaviors with your ideals.

If you're confused about what's truly important to you right now, you're not alone. In reality, few people take the time to pause and reflect on what matters most to them. It's like growing up with values imposed on us like stickers by others, leaving us confused about our own beliefs. Well, it's time to change that. It's time to discover who you are, what you believe in, what you stand for, and what makes you happy.

Exercise 21: Your 80th Birthday

This short exercise seeks to extract your most significant values by considering what you want others to say about you.

1. Imagine yourself celebrating your 80th birthday surrounded by loved ones, including people who may not be present in your life yet. For example, imagine a partner beside you if you're currently single. You can also imagine future children, grandchildren, or friends you may not have met yet. Picture the venue, the decorations, and the happy atmosphere. Take a moment to soak in the joyous occasion.

2. Imagine each person at your party standing up to say something about you. What do you wish they would say?

Example:
Person: future son or daughter

What I wish they would say: Dad, I love you. I cherish every moment you spent with me playing basketball, even though I knew you hated it! I can only hope to be as amazing a father to my son as you were to me.

Person:
What I wish they would say:

Person:
What I wish they would say:

Person:
What I wish they would say:

Person:
What I wish they would say:

3. **Reframe**. Reflect on the toasts you want to hear on your 80th birthday and reframe them into values. For example, suppose you wish your child (or future child) to say, "You were my best friend growing up, Dad. I couldn't ask for a better role model." This may translate into values such as, "As a parent, I want to listen and always be a part of my child's life."

Birthday wish: Value translation:
Birthday wish: Value translation:
Birthday wish:

Value translation:

Birthday wish:
Value translation:

Birthday wish:
Value translation:

4. **Value integration.** After imagining the toasts you want to hear on your 80th birthday and identifying the values they represent, the next step is to integrate those values into your daily life. Consider how you can prioritize these values in your day-to-day actions and decisions.

For example, suppose you want your child to say you were their best friend growing up. This can translate to personal values such as *presence, communication, friendship, trust, quality time*, etc. In that case, think of ways to foster these values now through your actions. For instance, the next time your child mentions a school event, actively listen to foster *communication* and prioritize attending to nurture *presence* and *quality time.*

Exercise 22: Values Discovery Journey

Even though you might not have taken a moment to deeply reflect and identify your values, it doesn't mean you've never lived according to at least some of them. This exercise aims to "open your eyes" to values you may have already prioritized by reflecting on past events that have brought you happiness.

1. **Reflect on past moments of happiness.** Think about a time when you felt truly happy and fulfilled. What were you doing? What values were you honoring in that moment?

   Example: I remember a time when I volunteered at a local animal shelter and felt a deep sense of joy and fulfillment.

2. **Recall decision points.** Remember a time when you were faced with a decision. What guided you to make the choice you did? What values were at play?

   Example: As a teen, I chose between a part-time job at a café that paid okay and a part-time job walking dogs that paid very little. I picked the second one.

```



```

3. **Envision your ideal future or your life in an alternate universe.** What are the most important things to you in that vision? What values do those things represent?

   Example: I see myself working as a vet. I associate this with values of compassion, empathy, responsibility, and respect for all living beings. It also probably means I value patience, understanding, and teamwork because I don't see myself working alone in my practice.

```



```

4. **Identify common themes.** Reflect on your answers from the previous steps and look for common themes or patterns. These can give you clues about your personal values. For example, if your answers involve "working with others," perhaps *connection,* a *sense of belonging,* and *community* are central to your identity.

5. **Prioritize the values you've identified** based on what feels most authentic and important to you. Consider which values you want to prioritize in your daily life and decision-making. For example, if you want to prioritize *connection* right now, seek daily opportunities to build better

friendships and relationships with others. For instance, you might want to improve your active listening skills and develop more empathy in communications.

Tip: Repeat this exercise to uncover more personal values.

Important: Prioritizing your values does not necessarily mean you need to change jobs and overhaul your life (unless this is what you want to do). Focusing on your values can also mean making daily decisions, even small ones, according to these values. For example, if you value *sustainability*, you might start by avoiding using plastic containers and bags from now on. You can level up later to lead a zero-waste life.

Exercise 23: Values Cards

In the previous exercise, you were asked to recall specific moments to see which values were important to you. In this exercise, you'll use Values Cards because they present ideals and principles you may not have previously considered. Here's how you can use a values card effectively:

1. Print out the Values table below and cut out each value. Please feel free to add more if you want to.

ADAPTABILITY	ADVENTURE	ALTRUISM
Being flexible and open to change, easily adjusting to new situations and circumstances.	Embracing new experiences, challenges, and opportunities for growth and exploration.	Acting selflessly and compassionately for the benefit of others without expecting anything in return.

AMBITION	AUTHENTICITY	AWARENESS
Setting high goals and aspirations and striving to achieve one's full potential.	Being true to oneself and living in alignment with one's values, beliefs, and identity.	Being conscious and attentive to oneself, others, and the environment, fostering mindfulness and insight.
BALANCE	**BEAUTY**	**CLARITY**
Finding equilibrium and harmony between various aspects of life, such as work, relationships, and self-care.	Appreciating and creating beauty in one's surroundings, experiences, and expressions.	Gaining a clear understanding and insight into one's values, goals, and priorities.
COLLABORATION	**COMMITMENT**	**COMMUNICATION**
Working cooperatively with others, sharing ideas, resources, and efforts to achieve common goals.	Dedication and loyalty to one's values, goals, and relationships, demonstrating steadfastness and perseverance.	Cultivating effective and empathetic communication skills to express oneself authentically, listen actively, and foster understanding and connection in relationships.
COMMUNITY	**COMPASSION**	**CONFIDENCE**
Fostering a sense of belonging and connection with others, supporting and being supported by a social network.	Showing kindness, empathy, and understanding towards oneself and others.	Believing in oneself and one's abilities and facing challenges with self-assurance and determination.

CONNECTION	**CONTENTMENT**	**COURAGE**
Building meaningful relationships and fostering a sense of belonging and community.	Finding satisfaction and peace with what I have and where I am in life.	Having the strength and bravery to face challenges, take risks, and pursue one's goals.
CREATIVITY	**CURIOSITY**	**DETERMINATION**
Expressing oneself through imagination, innovation, and originality.	Seeking knowledge, exploration, and new experiences, driven by a desire to learn and understand.	Having strong willpower and perseverance to overcome obstacles and achieve one's goals.
DISCIPLINE	**EMPOWERMENT**	**EQUANIMITY**
Maintaining self-control, focus, and dedication in pursuing one's objectives and commitments.	Taking control of one's life and choices and empowering oneself and others to thrive.	Maintaining emotional balance and composure in the face of challenges and fluctuations.
FAITH	**FLEXIBILITY**	**FREEDOM**
Trusting in a higher power, universal wisdom, or guiding principles, and surrendering to the flow of life.	Adapting to change, uncertainty, and challenges with openness, agility, and resilience.	Experiencing liberation from constraints, limitations, and fears, and living authentically and boldly.
GENEROSITY	**GRATITUDE**	**GROWTH**
Giving freely and generously of one's time, resources, and compassion to benefit	Appreciating the positive aspects of life and expressing thankfulness for blessings and	Continuously striving for personal and professional development, learning,

others.	opportunities.	and self-improvement.
HONESTY Truthfulness and sincerity in communication and interactions.	**HUMILITY** Cultivating modesty, open-mindedness, and a willingness to learn from others and life's experiences.	**HUMOR** Finding and sharing joy, laughter, and light-heartedness, even in difficult or serious situations.
INCLUSIVITY Embracing diversity and welcoming all individuals, regardless of differences or backgrounds.	**INDEPENDENCE** Asserting autonomy, self-reliance, and freedom of thought and action.	**INNOVATION** Embracing creativity and originality, generating new ideas and solutions to old problems.
INSPIRATION Igniting creativity, motivation, and passion through meaningful experiences and connections.	**INTEGRITY** Acting with honesty, ethics, and moral principles, and staying true to one's values.	**JOY** Finding happiness, pleasure, and fulfillment in life's experiences and moments.
JUSTICE Upholding fairness, equality, and righteousness in one's actions and interactions with others.	**KINDNESS** Showing generosity, compassion, and goodwill towards oneself and others.	**LOVE** Cultivating deep connections, affection, and care for oneself and others.
LOYALTY Being faithful, committed, and supportive to one's	**MEANING** Finding purpose, significance, and fulfillment in one's life	**MINDFULNESS** Being present in the moment, aware of one's thoughts, feelings, and

values, relationships, and responsibilities.	and experiences.	surroundings without judgment.
NURTURE Providing care, support, and nourishment to oneself and others for growth and well-being.	**OPENNESS** Embracing new ideas, perspectives, and experiences with curiosity, receptivity, and non-judgment.	**OPTIMISM** Maintaining a positive outlook and hopeful attitude towards the future, even in challenging times.
PATIENCE Practicing tolerance and acceptance of delays, difficulties, and imperfections, fostering endurance and calmness.	**PEACE** Cultivating inner calm, tranquility, and serenity amidst life's stresses and uncertainties.	**PERSISTENCE** Pursuing one's goals and dreams despite obstacles, setbacks, and failures.
PLAYFULNESS Embracing spontaneity, joy, and creativity, engaging in activities for sheer enjoyment and fun.	**PRESENCE** Being fully engaged and attentive in the here and now, and savoring each moment of life.	**PURPOSE** Living with intention, direction, and meaning, and aligning one's actions with one's values and goals.
REFLECTION Engaging in introspection and self-examination, learning from past experiences, and gaining insight into oneself.	**RESILIENCE** Bouncing back from adversity, setbacks, and hardships with strength, adaptability, and determination.	**SELF-COMPASSION** Treating oneself with kindness, understanding, and forgiveness in times of difficulty or suffering.
SELF-DISCIPLINE	**SELF-EXPRESSION**	**SERVICE**

Exercising control and restraint over one's impulses and behaviors, staying focused on long-term goals.	Expressing one's thoughts, feelings, and identity authentically and creatively through various forms of communication and expression.	Contributing to the well-being and happiness of others through acts of service, generosity, and kindness.
SIMPLICITY Embracing a minimalist lifestyle and mindset, focusing on what truly matters, and letting go of excess or unnecessary distractions.	**SOBRIETY** Maintaining abstinence or moderation from substances or behaviors that can impair judgment, health, or well-being.	**SPIRITUALITY** Connecting with something greater than oneself, exploring beliefs and practices that provide meaning and purpose.
STABILITY Cultivating a sense of security, predictability, and steadiness in one's life and environment.	**SUSTAINABILITY** Promoting environmental stewardship and responsible living, ensuring the well-being of future generations.	**TEAMWORK** Collaborating with others towards shared goals, mutual support, and collective success.
TENACITY Demonstrating determination, perseverance, and resilience in pursuing one's objectives and aspirations.	**TRANSPARENCY** Practicing honesty, openness, and authenticity in one's communications and interactions.	**TRUST** Having confidence in oneself, others, and the universe, and believing in the inherent goodness of life.
UNITY Fostering harmony, cohesion, and solidarity	**VITALITY** Nurturing energy, vigor, and vitality in one's	**WISDOM** Cultivating insight, discernment, and practical

among individuals and communities despite differences or disagreements.	physical, mental, and emotional well-being.	knowledge to navigate life's challenges and complexities.
Add another value you want here…	*Add another value you want here…*	*Add another value you want here…*
Add another value you want here…	*Add another value you want here…*	*Add another value you want here…*

2. **Select your values.** Spread the Values cards before you, ensuring you can see all the options. Take the time and review each value carefully. Next, select the values that resonate most deeply with you.

3. **Reflect.** Once you've selected your values, think about why you chose those particular values.

- Explore how these values align with your goals, dreams, and overall sense of fulfillment. For example, suppose you identified *adventure* as a core value because you love exploring new places and trying new experiences. As you explore how this value aligns with your goals and dreams, you might realize that it fuels your desire to travel the world and seek out exciting opportunities for personal growth. You feel most fulfilled when embarking on adventures that push you out of your comfort zone and expand your horizons.

- Reflect on past experiences when you lived in alignment with these values and how they affected your well-being. For instance, suppose you have always valued *kindness* because you believe in treating others with compassion and empathy. As you reflect on past experiences when you lived in alignment with this value, you remember how volunteering at a homeless shelter brought you a sense of fulfillment and purpose. You realize that acts of *kindness* benefit others and contribute to your sense of well-being and fulfillment.

4. **Prioritize your values.** After selecting and reflecting on your values, prioritize them based on their significance and importance. For each value you consider a top priority, ask yourself why?

Example:
Top priority value: trust
Why: I don't want to second guess or doubt my motives or those of others.

Top priority:
Why?

Top priority:
Why?

Top priority:
Why?

5. **Setting goals and taking action.** Use the values you identified as input for goal-setting and action planning. Use the **SMART** technique as defined in ACT (**S**pecific, **M**eaningful, **A**daptive, **R**ealistic, **T**ime-Bound).

Value to prioritize:

Example: honesty

Specific. Clearly define what this value means to you and how you want to incorporate it into your life.

Example: Honesty is extremely important to me, so I will start with myself. I've always struggled to be honest with my parents. I don't always agree with them, but I just give in instead of disagreeing and giving my opinion. From now on, I'll strive to always tell the truth, even when it's difficult.

Meaningful. Why are you doing this? What's the meaning of this goal to you?

Example: I'm tired of giving in and feeling like I never have a voice with my parents. I'm an adult, but I feel like a child with them. Being able to be honest with them means that I'm standing my ground and being authentic.

Adaptive. Do you believe this goal will help you achieve a value-based life? How so?

Example: Yes! If I'm authentic with my parents, I can also strive to be authentic in other areas of my life.

Realistic. Is this goal realistically achievable?

Example: I believe so.

Time-bound: Establish a timeline for achieving your goals. Set deadlines for specific actions or milestones.

Example: Starting next week, I will be honest in all conversations with my parents. I will monitor this in my journal for at least three months.

Important: Regularly review your values and goals to ensure they're aligned with each other. Sometimes, you may realize that you're not prioritizing your most important values or that your goals are not aligned with your values. That's okay. Reflect and adjust, and keep moving forward.

Exercise 24: Values Bull's Eye

This exercise aims to help you identify and prioritize your core values in the following areas of your life: relationships, work, personal growth, and leisure.

1. **Find a quiet and comfortable space** where you can reflect without distractions. Take a few deep breaths to center yourself and clear your mind.

2. Reflect on the following aspects of your life: *relationships, work, personal growth (health)*, and *leisure*. Consider what is truly important to you in each of these areas. If helpful, reflect on past experiences or moments when you felt most fulfilled and aligned with your values in these areas.

3. Take a piece of paper and brainstorm a list of values that resonate with you. Write down any words or phrases that come to mind without censoring yourself. Consider tangible and intangible values like honesty, creativity, family, health, and adventure. **Tip:** Use the Values cards from the previous exercise.

4. Prioritize your values and identify the **Top 25** that resonate most with you. Rank these values in order of importance, with the most important value at the top and the least important at the bottom.

5. From your Top 25 Values, take your "Value Priority #1" and refer to the Values bull's eye diagram below. Pick a section and ask yourself, "Am I living my life fully by this value in this aspect?" Place an "x" near the circle's center (red area) if you live according to your value. If not, place an "x" away from the center (outer circles).

Move on to the next section and ask the same question. Keep going till you go through all four areas of your life.

Here's an example using the value "balance."

In *relationships*, balance means maintaining healthy boundaries, giving and receiving support equally, and prioritizing quality time with loved ones while nurturing independence and individual growth.

In your *work* life, balance involves finding harmony between work and personal life, avoiding burnout, and pursuing opportunities for growth and development while enjoying downtime and leisure activities.

In *personal growth*, balance entails striving for growth and improvement while accepting oneself and practicing self-care. It involves setting goals and challenges while allowing time for reflection, relaxation, and enjoyment.

In leisure activities, balance means engaging in various activities that bring joy and fulfillment while also making time for rest and relaxation. It involves pursuing hobbies and interests that nourish the mind, body, and soul without overcommitting or neglecting other aspects of life.

Here's a sample Values Bull's Eye diagram with the above definitions of what "balance" means in various life aspects.

Value: BALANCE

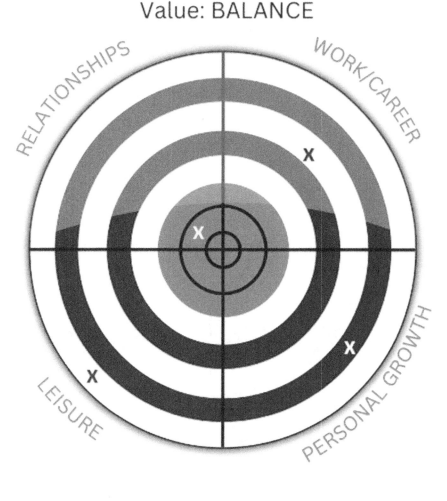

It's your turn to fill out the diagram using the image below.

Value: _____

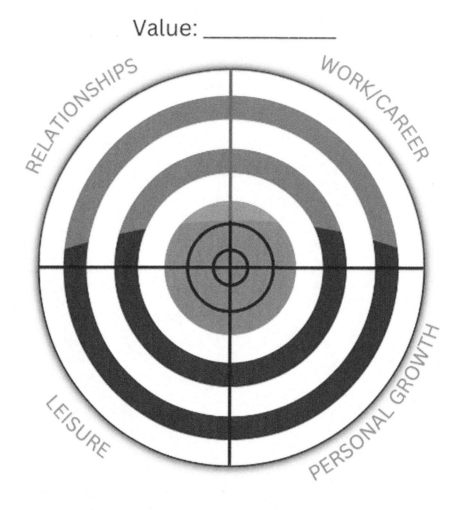

6. **Reflect on alignment.** Look at the diagram you created. Reflect on how well your current lifestyle aligns with a specific value. Are you living by it, or are there areas where you could make adjustments to better align with what matters most to you?

7. **Set value-based goals.** If you notice one life aspect where you're not living fully according to a value, plan and set goals to change that. For example, suppose you're not achieving "balance" in *leisure*. Perhaps you're overcommitting and trying to find time to engage in sports with different groups of friends several times a week and then with your partner on the

weekends. In this case, you might want to lessen your weekly commitments so that you (and your body) have time for rest and relaxation.

Chapter 8: Committed Action

In ACT, a life of unhappiness and internal distress is often due to a *misalignment* between your values and actions. For example, if one values *commitment* yet lives a life of procrastination, inconsistency, and indecision, it can lead to inner conflict and dissatisfaction. Similarly, suppose someone values *authenticity* but constantly suppresses their true thoughts and feelings to fit in. In that case, they may experience a sense of disconnection and lack of fulfillment.

So, the key to living a more meaningful and fulfilling life lies in identifying your core values and aligning your actions with them. And yes, that's easier said than done.

Behavioral change is difficult.[36,37] For example, as you read this, you might already think about all the challenges and difficulties you will face. You might even wonder if you have it in you to succeed. In ACT, these psychological barriers to change are called FEAR.

- **F**usion. This is when you struggle with negative thinking, anticipating how your plans could fail or appear unachievable. Before you even begin, you might think this "living according to my values" thing is too tough for you.

- **E**xcessive goal making. Setting goals that exceed your existing resources (e.g., skills, time, money, etc.) might result in swift failure or giving up entirely. Setting realistic goals that correspond to your abilities and available resources is critical.

- **A**voidance of discomfort. Change inevitably brings discomfort, often in the form of anxiety or other challenging emotions. If you're unwilling to tolerate this discomfort, you might stay with what's familiar (comfort zone), even though this doesn't help you achieve your value-based goals.

- **R**emoteness from values. Before you start identifying and working on your goals, ensure they align with YOUR values. Sometimes, our goals are not aligned with our deepest values but rather influenced by external forces (i.e., family, society, what's viral and trending, etc.). If this is the case, it's easier to give up because, well, it's easier to do so when it comes to things we don't truly care about.

Although having doubts and questions (FEAR) is normal, it doesn't mean you cannot succeed. The solution to FEAR is DARE.

- **D**efusion. As mentioned in Chapter 5: Cognitive Defusion (a.k.a. Unhooking), defusion is about identifying the negative and unhelpful thoughts holding you back in life and unhooking yourself from them.

- **A**cceptance. Do not avoid or deny your painful and unhelpful thoughts and emotions. Accept that they exist so that you can move on from them.

- **R**ealistic aims. If you have a goal for which you do not have the necessary resources, then you have two options. First, you can start with the goal of acquiring the necessary resources you need. For example, if you want to advance at work but need more leadership skills, your first goal should be to acquire these skills. Second, if the necessary resources are unavailable, accept reality's current constraints and modify your goals.

- **E**mbrace your true values. If you find yourself uncommitted or unmotivated about your goals, consider whether the "value" you're attempting to uphold is genuinely important to you. Is this your value or someone else's? If you think the value is important to you, is the action you've chosen to take really connected to it?

Committed action in ACT is acknowledging the existence of FEAR but embracing DARE. It's about taking meaningful steps towards living a life that aligns with your values, even in the face of difficult emotions or challenging circumstances. It is the opposite of *delay* or *avoidance.* It's about making deliberate choices, taking intentional actions, and consistently showing up and engaging in behaviors that align with your values. Further, committed action is not about "thinking" about taking action; it's about taking real action in the real world.

Setting Goals... and Actually Accomplishing Them

According to Russ Harris, author of *The Happiness Trap*[38] and a proponent of ACT, there are four steps to steps to committed action:

Step 1. Choose a life domain that is a high priority for change. Identify an area of your life where you feel dissatisfied or desire improvement. For example, you might choose your *work life* or *career* if you feel unfulfilled or stagnant in your current job.

Step 2. Choose what values you wish to pursue in this domain. Determine the core values that are important to you in your chosen domain.

These values represent what truly matters to you in that area of your life. For example, if you choose your career, your values might include *creativity, growth, making a positive impact*, etc.

Step 3. Develop goals that are guided by those values. Set <u>SMART</u> (<u>S</u>pecific, <u>M</u>eaningful, <u>A</u>daptive, <u>R</u>ealistic, <u>T</u>ime-Bound) goals that align with your chosen values. These goals should reflect the kind of life you want to live in that domain. Using the career example, if your value is *creativity*, your goal might be to *pursue a job that allows you to express your creativity regularly*.

Step 4. Take action mindfully. Actively engage in activities that move you closer to your goals while staying present and aware of your thoughts, feelings, and sensations. In short, as you engage in an activity, be 100% present in that moment. Don't think of the past or the future; just be in NOW. For example, suppose your goal is to be more creative at work. In this case, you might take mindful action by brainstorming new ideas during team meetings and being fully present and attentive to the creative process.

Exercise 25: Committed Action

In this exercise, you will apply the four steps of "committed action."

Step 1. Identify the life domain that is a high priority for change. Note that you might need to break down this particular aspect of your life further and assess which one(s) have priority.

Example:
Life domain: relationships
Particular aspects: romantic relationships, friendships, family connections, professional relationships
Priority for change: family connections

Life domain:
Priority for change:
Priority for change:

Step 2. Choose what values you wish to pursue in this domain.

Example:

Life domain: relationships

Priority for change: family connections

Values: honesty, trust, communication, respect, empathy, support

Step 3. Develop goals that are guided by those values. Based on your prioritized values, brainstorm specific goals you want to achieve in this domain. Remember, your goals should be in alignment with your values. Use the SMART (**S**pecific, **M**eaningful, **A**daptive, **R**ealistic, **T**ime-Bound) technique.

Life domain: _____ *Example: relationships*
Priority for change: _____ *Example: family connections*
Value to prioritize: _____ *Example: communication, harmony*

Specific. What are your specific goals regarding this value? Be as detailed as possible.

Example:

- *I will improve communication with my siblings by regularly asking them for lunch. Preferably, at least one lunch date every other week.*
- *I will start my invites next week, for Saturday, 12 noon, at Café ACT.*
- *If one can't make it, I will NOT cancel and still hold the lunch date with those who can.*
- *I will not be discouraged if an intended lunch date doesn't push through. We all have busy lives, after all. Instead, I will ask them out again the following week.*
- *I accept that I have no control over the conversation during these lunches. There will be times when it's all fun and when we disagree with each other. I will do my best to practice patience and open-mindedness and encourage them to do the same.*

Meaningful. Why are you doing this? What's the meaning of this goal to you?

Example: I want to communicate better with my siblings because we're always getting into misunderstandings over the most trivial things! And yet, even though they're trivial, I feel enormous sadness and anxiety over them.

Adaptive. Do you believe this goal will help you achieve a value-based life in this domain? How so?

Example: Yes. By fostering more and better communication with my siblings, I believe there will be fewer misunderstandings between us, which is better for my mental well-being.

Realistic. Is this goal realistically achievable?

Example: I believe so. We all live in the same city, so meeting for lunch every other week or once a month is possible. We also all have jobs, so paying for lunch shouldn't be a problem.

Time-bound. Establish a timeline for achieving your goals. Set deadlines for specific actions or milestones.

Example:

- *I will start my invites next week, for Saturday, 12 noon, at Café ACT.*
- *I will initiate these lunch dates for at least three months.*
- *After three months, I'll assess if our communication and harmony have improved.*

Step 4. Take action mindfully. Practice present-moment awareness while engaging in the activities that enable you to achieve your value-based goal.

Example: I will treat these lunch dates with my siblings as "sacred time." No answering calls, no checking of emails, etc. I will actively listen when someone speaks and politely ask them to do the same when I have something to share.

```



```

Exercise 26: Values-Based Exposure

In the previous exercise, you identified your life values and listed the steps you want to take to live according to them. Good for you!

Now, there might be times when certain goals require you to confront uncomfortable or even feared situations. For example, you might need to assert yourself in a challenging conversation at work to uphold your value of *honesty,* or you might need to push through your fear of public speaking to pursue your value of *making a difference in your community.* This is where Values-Based Exposure (VBE) comes in handy. It will help you face your fears while staying true to your values.

1. **Identify your value-based goal.** Start by identifying the goal you want to achieve.

   Example: I want to be better at initiating conversations.

```



```

>

2. Identify the values associated with your goal.

Examples: connection, communication, authenticity, courage, growth

>

3. **Choose a target situation.** Choose a specific situation or scenario where you struggle to initiate conversations due to anxiety, fear, low self-esteem, etc. This could be initiating conversations with strangers, colleagues, acquaintances, or potential friends. Start with a situation that feels challenging but manageable.

Example: Initiate a conversation with a co-worker I like.

> Target situation:

4. **Set clear action steps.** How do you intend to meet your goal? Be clear and specific with what you intend to do. For example, your goal might be to initiate a conversation with at least three new people in a social setting within the next week. Make sure your goals are realistic and achievable within your current comfort level.

Action steps:

---

5. **Prepare mindfully.** Prepare yourself mentally and emotionally for the exposure exercise. Practice mindfulness techniques to stay present and grounded in the moment.

6. **Visualize success.** Take some time to visualize yourself successfully doing your action steps. For example, if one of your action steps is to talk to three strangers today, imagine yourself feeling confident, relaxed, and engaged as you approach others and start conversations. Visualizing success can help build confidence and reduce anxiety.

7. **Begin with small, low-pressure exposure tasks.** Take small steps to gradually build confidence and momentum. For example, suppose your objective is to be better at initiating conversations. In that case, you might want to start with initiating very brief conversations with people you encounter in everyday situations, such as asking a cashier how their day is going or complimenting a coworker on their work.

8. **Challenge avoidant behaviors.** Identify any avoidance behaviors you engage in to avoid doing what you set out to do. For example, if you're uncomfortable initiating conversations, you might often avoid eye contact, stay glued to your phone, or leave social situations early. If so, challenge

yourself to gradually reduce these avoidance behaviors during the exposure exercise by planning ahead.

AVOIDANT BEHAVIOR	PLAN
Example: I usually avoid eye contact.	*Example: Practice making brief, intentional eye contact with people in low-stress situations, such as with friends or family.*

9. **Accept discomfort.** Accept that discomfort and anxiety are normal parts of the exposure process. Instead of trying to avoid or suppress these feelings, practice willingness to experience them fully while still acting in line with your values. (**Tip**: Try Willing Hands.) Remind yourself that feeling discomfort is normal, but it is temporary.

10. **Remember your values.** Reflect on how the activity aligns with your values throughout the exposure exercise. Notice how participating in the activity brings a sense of fulfillment, even if they feel challenging or uncomfortable in the moment.

11. **Celebrate successes.** Celebrate each success and milestone you achieve during the exposure exercise, no matter how small. Acknowledge your courage and progress in facing your fears and taking steps toward your goals. Reward yourself with self-care activities or positive affirmations to reinforce your efforts!

12. **Reflect and adjust.** After completing the exposure exercise, reflect on your experience and what you've learned. Identify any insights or lessons gained from the process and areas for improvement or adjustment. Use this feedback to refine your approach and set new goals for future exposure exercises.

Exercise 27: Living in the Future

As you engage in "committed action," it's normal to experience setbacks. However, the key to success is to "keep your eye on the ball." That is, you must not lose sight of what you're trying to achieve, and one of the best ways to do that is to visualize yourself in the future, living your value-based life.

1. **Find a quiet and comfortable space** where you won't be disturbed. Close your eyes and take a few slow, deep breaths to **center yourself**.

2. **Bring to mind a valued intention or goal** that you've been working towards. It could be anything from improving relationships to advancing your career or personal well-being. Visualize this goal clearly in your mind.

3. **Envision yourself successfully living out this value or intention.** Picture yourself taking action in alignment with this value, with no

obstacles standing in your way. Imagine feeling confident, capable, and fulfilled as you pursue your goals.

4. **Pay attention to how it feels to succeed in this area of your life.** Notice any feelings of satisfaction, pride, or contentment within you. Allow yourself to fully **immerse in the positive emotions associated with living according to your values**.

5. Take a moment to acknowledge any thoughts, emotions, or physical sensations that arise during this visualization. **Notice how your body and mind respond to the experience of success and fulfillment.**

6. **Shift your focus to the external environment in your visualization.** Notice any changes in the world around you resulting from achieving your goal. For example, suppose your goal was to improve communication and connection with your partner. In this case, imagine your relationship now that you've achieved this goal.

7. Take as much time as you need to **fully immerse yourself in this visualization** and experience the rewards of living in alignment with your values. When you're ready to conclude the exercise, slowly open your eyes.

8. Grab a pen, a piece of paper, or a journal, and jot down all the positive outcomes and insights you discovered during this exercise. Reflect on how you can carry these lessons forward and continue to pursue your values with clarity and purpose.

Part 3: Moving Forward with ACT

"Challenges are what make life interesting, and overcoming them is what makes life meaningful." – Joshua J. Marine

Chapter 9: ACT Maintenance and Growth

As you continue your journey with ACT, focusing on maintenance and growth is essential to sustain your progress and further enhance your psychological flexibility. Remember that, as with any life skill, you need to consistently apply what you've learned until it becomes a habit.

The following exercises explore strategies for deepening your understanding of yourself and your values and how you can further integrate ACT principles into your daily life.

Exercise 28: Your Life Compass

This exercise helps you continually live a life of value-based intention and purpose. It allows you to look at your life and all its aspects— *family, intimate relationships, work or career, health, leisure, social life, education, and spirituality*—the core values you want to apply to them and reflect on your desired life direction.

1. Each box below represents an aspect of your life. In each box, write down:

   - The values most important to you.
   - The people who matter most.

- Who you want to be.
- Your current strengths and qualities.
- Other strengths, qualities, or skills you want to develop or acquire.
- Your goals.

Note: If a box feels irrelevant right now, leave it blank and return to it whenever you feel it's appropriate. It's fine if the same words appear in multiple boxes; this can help you pinpoint essential values.

2. **Priority.** After completing all the boxes, rate each box according to their priority in your life.

3. **Values adherence.** After completing all the boxes, return to the first box and reflect on the values you wrote down. Next, rate your current level of adherence to these values on a scale of 0 to 10, with 0=not adhering at all and 10 for extremely adhering.

4. After rating your value adherence for all the boxes, reflect on what you wrote.

- What is this Life Compass exercise telling you?
- Based on your rating, what are the most essential aspects of your life?
- Are you living according to your life priorities?
- Say you prioritize "Family" above all. What's your value adherence rating for that life aspect? Are you content or happy with this self-rating? If so, do you have any other goals you wish to add? If not, review or revise your goals.

Here's an example:

FAMILY	Priority: 2
Values: love, respect, communication, support, unity, compassion, forgiveness, responsibility, acknowledgment, gratitude	**Adherence: 6**
People who matter most: mom, dad, siblings, and grandma Ellie	
Who I want to be: I want to be part of my family again. I left home early, and it seemed like I left and never looked back. I want to change that.	
Current strengths and qualities: I'm a committed person. I'm also loving even though I don't always show it. I can also be very giving.	
Strengths, qualities, and skills I want to develop: Better communication, more time for family, gratitude.	
Immediate goals. Something modest, basic, and achievable within the next 24 hours. <ul><li>Call mom!</li><li>Ask if I can visit next weekend.</li></ul>	
Short-term goals. Targets that can be accomplished within the next few days or weeks. <ul><li>Visit family and STAY the whole weekend.</li></ul>	
Medium-term goals. Targets that can be completed during the following few weeks or months. <ul><li>Stay in touch. Call my parents every weekend.</li><li>Invite my sisters to visit me this summer.</li></ul>	
Long-term goals. Targets that will be achieved in the following months or years. <ul><li>Improve my relationship with my parents.</li><li>Build my non-existent relationship with my older and younger sisters.</li></ul>	

Now, it's your turn.

FAMILY	Priority:
Values:	**Adherence:**

People who matter most:

Who I want to be:

Current strengths and qualities:

Strengths, qualities, skills I want to develop:

Immediate goals.
Something modest, basic, and achievable within the next 24 hours.

Short-term goals.
Targets that can be accomplished within the next few days or weeks.

Medium-term goals.
Targets that can be completed during the following few weeks or months.

Long-term goals.

Targets that will be achieved in the following months or years.

INTIMATE RELATIONSHIPS	Priority:
Values:	**Adherence:**

People who matter most:

Who I want to be:

Current strengths and qualities:

Strengths, qualities, skills I want to develop:

Immediate goals.
Something modest, basic, and achievable within the next 24 hours.

Short-term goals.

Targets that can be accomplished within the next few days or weeks.

Medium-term goals.
Targets that can be completed during the following few weeks or months.

Long-term goals.
Targets that will be achieved in the following months or years.

WORK | JOB | CAREER	Priority:
Values:	Adherence:
People who matter most:	
Who I want to be:	

Current strengths and qualities:

Strengths, qualities, skills I want to develop:

Immediate goals.
Something modest, basic, and achievable within the next 24 hours.

Short-term goals.
Targets that can be accomplished within the next few days or weeks.

Medium-term goals.
Targets that can be completed during the following few weeks or months.

Long-term goals.
Targets that will be achieved in the following months or years.

HEALTH (Mental, Physical, and Emotional)	Priority:
Values:	Adherence:
People who matter most:	
Who I want to be:	
Current strengths and qualities:	
Strengths, qualities, skills I want to develop:	
Immediate goals. *Something modest, basic, and achievable within the next 24 hours.*	
Short-term goals. *Targets that can be accomplished within the next few days or weeks.*	

<table>
<tr><td colspan="2"></td></tr>
<tr><td colspan="2">Medium-term goals.
Targets that can be completed during the following few weeks or months.</td></tr>
<tr><td colspan="2">Long-term goals.
Targets that will be achieved in the following months or years.</td></tr>
</table>

RECREATION | LEISURE	Priority:
Values:	**Adherence:**
People who matter most:	
Who I want to be:	
Current strengths and qualities:	

Strengths, qualities, skills I want to develop:

Immediate goals.
Something modest, basic, and achievable within the next 24 hours.

Short-term goals.
Targets that can be accomplished within the next few days or weeks.

Medium-term goals.
Targets that can be completed during the following few weeks or months.

Long-term goals.
Targets that will be achieved in the following months or years.

SOCIAL LIFE	Priority:

Values:	Adherence:

People who matter most:

Who I want to be:

Current strengths and qualities:

Strengths, qualities, skills I want to develop:

Immediate goals.
Something modest, basic, and achievable within the next 24 hours.

Short-term goals.
Targets that can be accomplished within the next few days or weeks.

Medium-term goals.
Targets that can be completed during the following few weeks or months.

Long-term goals.
Targets that will be achieved in the following months or years.

SCHOOL | EDUCATION	Priority:
Values:	**Adherence:**

People who matter most:

Who I want to be:

Current strengths and qualities:

Strengths, qualities, skills I want to develop:

Immediate goals.
Something modest, basic, and achievable within the next 24 hours.

Short-term goals.
Targets that can be accomplished within the next few days or weeks.

Medium-term goals.
Targets that can be completed during the following few weeks or months.

Long-term goals.
Targets that will be achieved in the following months or years.

FAITH	SPIRITUALITY	Priority:
Values:	Adherence:

People who matter most:
Who I want to be:
Current strengths and qualities:
Strengths, qualities, skills I want to develop:
Immediate goals. *Something modest, basic, and achievable within the next 24 hours.*
Short-term goals. *Targets that can be accomplished within the next few days or weeks.*
Medium-term goals. *Targets that can be completed during the following few weeks or months.*
Long-term goals.

> *Targets that will be achieved in the following months or years.*

After doing this activity, print it out and keep it. During tough or challenging moments, take it out to remind yourself of your values and your life goals. It will help you "stay true" during challenging times.

Also, life is ever-changing. Your priorities, the values you associate with them, and your goals might change, so it's good to reflect and re-evaluate every now and then.

Chapter 10: Self-Guided ACT

You have learned A LOT, delving deep into the principles of ACT and gaining invaluable insights into yourself. Feeling overwhelmed and perhaps even inclined to take a break and let everything sink in is normal.

When you're ready to dive back in, you might be unsure where to begin. That's why I've crafted a special 30-day ACT Plan to guide you on your continued journey of growth and self-discovery.

Exercise 29: Your 30-Day ACT Plan

This 30-day ACT plan is a guide. Its goal is progress, not perfection. So, keep to the plan as much as possible, but if setbacks happen, that's okay. Just get back up and keep on going!

Week 1: Building Awareness and Acceptance

Days 1-3:

☐ **Day 1:** Spend at least 10 minutes practicing mindfulness, focusing on your breath or body sensations. (**Tip:** Select any of the mindfulness exercises mentioned in Chapter 4: Mindfulness (Present Moment Awareness)

☐ **Day 2:** Engage in mindfulness and notice any negative thoughts or emotions that arise during the day without judgment. Accept these thoughts AS IS. (**Tip:** If you find yourself resisting acceptance, re-read Chapter 3: Acceptance.)

☐ **Day 3:** Write down three things you struggle to accept about yourself or your life and reflect on how these things might be holding you back or keeping you in a cage of unhappiness. Reflect on how acceptance can free you from mental and emotional suffering.

Days 4-7: Start practicing cognitive defusion.

☐ **Day 4:** Reflect on any negative thoughts you might be having about yourself and then label them as "Thoughts." Remind yourself that you are not your thoughts. They are not facts. Your thoughts are mental events coming and going like clouds in the sky. (**Tip:** Experiment with techniques from Chapter 5: Cognitive Defusion (a.k.a. Unhooking) and find what works best for you.)

☐ **Day 5:** Engage in a pleasant activity mindfully, paying attention to the sensations and emotions it brings. Notice how doing the things you love or are passionate about brings you joy. If you observe unhelpful thoughts, practice cognitive defusion and let these thoughts pass without judgment.

☐ **Day 6:** If any negative or unhelpful thoughts arise, distract yourself by making it a game and using the Defusion Wheel exercise. Notice how distancing yourself from difficult emotions or situations makes you feel better, allowing you to move forward.

☐ **Day 7:** Journal and list down your unique skills and positive qualities. If any negative thoughts arise, don't try to deny it or push it away. Instead, say aloud, "Ah, I'm having this thought that I'm _____." Then, mentally place the thought outside yourself, like putting it in a box and visualizing placing that box in another room.

Week 2: Clarifying Values

Day 8-10:

☐ **Day 8:** Randomly pick one of the "life boxes" you filled out in the Life Compass exercise in the previous chapter. Are you living in alignment with the values you wrote in this box? If not, think of ways to align your daily decisions and actions with the values you indicated in the "life box" you chose.

☐ **Day 9:** Randomly choose one value to focus on today and set one small, meaningful act or goal related to it. For example, suppose you picked the value *discipline"* In this case, a small goal might be to ensure you drink 8 glasses of water today.

☐ **Day 10:** Randomly choose one value to focus on today and set one small, meaningful act or goal related to it. However, this time, involve others. They don't need to know what you're doing. The objective is to extend the value to others. For example, suppose you picked the value of *kindness*. In this case, a small goal might be to genuinely smile at three people today or do a small favor for someone.

Days 11-14:

☐ **Day 11:** Practice kindness and self-compassion to yourself today. Acknowledge and soothe any pain or difficulties you may be going through.

☐ **Day 12:** Notice any behaviors driven by fear or avoidance, and consider how they conflict with your values. For example, suppose you're avoiding talking to a friend with whom you recently had a misunderstanding. In that case, you might be going against values such as *communication, connection,* and *forgiveness.*

☐ **Day 13:** Pick an important personal value. Take one small action aligned with your chosen value, even if it feels uncomfortable.

☐ **Day 14:** Pick an important personal value. (You can use the same one as yesterday's.) Take one small action aligned with your chosen value, even if it feels uncomfortable. Reflect on how it felt to act per your values. Did it bring a sense of fulfillment or purpose?

Week 3: Committed Action

Days 15-17:

☐ **Day 15:** Set aside time to create a **SMART** (**S**pecific, **M**eaningful, **A**daptive, **R**ealistic, **T**ime-Bound) goal related to a value you've identified.

☐ **Day 16:** Break down your value-based SMART goal into smaller action steps and schedule them throughout the week.

☐ **Day 17:** Practice self-compassion and acceptance if you encounter obstacles or setbacks in pursuing your goal.

Day 18-21:

☐ **Day 18:** Engage in a mindfulness exercise to connect with yourself today.

- ☐ **Day 19:** Take action on one of the steps you identified on Day 15, even if it's challenging.
- ☐ **Day 20:** Notice any internal barriers (e.g., self-doubt, fear) that arise and practice acceptance of these feelings.
- ☐ **Day 21:** Reflect on any progress on your SMART goal and celebrate your achievements, no matter how small.

Week 4: Integration and Maintenance

Days 22-24:

- ☐ **Day 22:** Review your values and goals and consider if any adjustments are needed based on your experiences. (**Tip:** Reflect on Chapter 7: Values Clarification and Chapter 8: Committed Action.)
- ☐ **Day 23:** Engage in a values-based activity that brings you joy or fulfillment.
- ☐ **Day 24:** Practice gratitude by reflecting on three things you're grateful for.

Days 25-28:

- ☐ **Day 25:** Revisit your mindfulness practice and spend 15 minutes in mindful awareness.
- ☐ **Day 26:** Reflect on how your relationship with difficult thoughts and emotions has shifted since starting this journey.
- ☐ **Day 27:** Write a letter to yourself, acknowledging your efforts and commitment to growth.
- ☐ **Day 28:** Plan for ongoing practice beyond the 30 days, setting intentions for continuing to integrate ACT principles into your life.

Day 29-30: Reflection and Celebration

- ☐ **Day 29:** Spend time reflecting on your 30-day journey with ACT. What have you learned about yourself? What changes have you noticed?

☐ **Day 30:** Celebrate your accomplishments and commit to ongoing growth and self-compassion. Consider sharing your experience with a supportive friend or journaling about your insights.

Conclusion

"Healing may not be so much about getting better as about letting go of everything that isn't you – all of the expectations, all of the beliefs – and becoming who you are." – Rachel Naomi Remen

Life can be overwhelming at times. It's full of ups and downs. Now, the "ups" are great, but when the "downs" occur, that's when you need to have *psychological flexibility*. When you can sway with the wind, roll with the punches, and stand up and adapt, that's when you thrive.

Our thoughts are very powerful. What we think we become. And I think this is where we often trip ourselves in life. We don't realize that the "Thought" stage is not yet the "Fact" stage, yet we behave as though it were. As such, our thoughts become a self-fulling prophecy.

Now, if the thoughts are positive and helpful, great! (That's why positive affirmations work.[39]) However, when our thoughts are unhelpful, painful, negative, or harmful, we set ourselves up for an unhappy life.

When people ask about ACT, I tell them I learned it in therapy. However, I also told them that I think ACT skills benefit anyone and everyone at any time in their lives. Why? We cannot erase stress, problems, and challenges. They are inherent to the human experience. However, these events don't have to overwhelm us or knock us to the ground. We can just... sway, stand right back up tall, and keep moving forward.

Here's a quick recap of ACT:

In Part 1: Acceptance and Commitment Therapy 101, you learned about the history of ACT, what it's all about, and how it can help you find relief from your current life situation. You also learned how to prepare yourself for your ACT self-guided practice.

In Part 2: the Six Core Principles of ACT, you discovered the skills you need to develop to foster psychological flexibility.

- **Acceptance** is learning to acknowledge your current situation AS IS without trying to control, evaluate, or judge it. You learned that Acceptance is the door that opens your life to change.

- **Mindfulness** is present-moment awareness. It's living in NOW and not feeling, thinking, and behaving based on the past or the future.

- **Cognitive Defusion** involves letting go of negative self-talk and beliefs. It's about unhooking, ungluing, and distancing yourself from unhelpful thoughts or stories you associate with yourself.

- **Self as Context** teaches you to be an "observer" of your thoughts instead of being controlled by them.

- **Values Clarification** is taking a step back and evaluating what YOU truly consider important in this life. It's time for self-discovery and life realignment.

- **Committed Action** is about taking concrete, intentional steps to live a value-based life. It's taking real action in the real world to live life according to your values.

In Part 3: Moving Forward with ACT, you were given the tools to help you maintain and sustain the progress you've made with ACT.

Psychological flexibility. I often think about what that phrase means to me.

When I started my journey, I just wanted all the negative stuff (e.g., pain, depression, loneliness, feelings of inadequacy, confusion, etc.) to STOP overwhelming me. But when I got to *cognitive defusion* and *values* clarification, my life opened up. All of a sudden, I had clarity.

I learned that I was unnecessarily attached to unhelpful (and, in many instances, even *false*) ideas about myself, and I needed to distance and release these beliefs from my being. I also shockingly discovered I was not living up to my values or what I considered important. I was living based on what others wanted and expected. I was living *their* values. No wonder I was so confused and unhappy!

Ultimately, I can only be grateful for what I've learned. Why? Because now, I'm happily living the life I truly want to live. I sincerely hope that you achieve the same.

A Little Help?

Dear Reader,

I hope this ACT workbook has positively influenced your mental and emotional healing journey. When I was suffering from burnout and a breakdown, "help" was a distant concept, and I felt lost in a maze of overwhelming emotions. But through the principles of ACT, I found a guiding light, and I hope you have too.

Many people don't realize how hard it is to get reviews and how much they help us authors. So, I would be incredibly grateful if you could take just a few seconds to write a short review about this book on Amazon, even if it's just a few words.

What to do: Please visit this link https://life-zen.com/actreview to leave a review on Amazon or scan the QR code on this page.

Note: If you're from outside the US, please update the link above from amazon.com to your country code (e.g., amazon.co.uk, amazon.ca, etc.).

If you're reading on a Kindle or an e-reader, scroll to the bottom of the book and swipe up to prompt the Review page.

THANK YOU FOR YOUR HELP!

Ava Watters

Further Reading

If you're struggling with practicing Acceptance and want help from someone who knows exactly what you're going through, please let me share my journey with you through this Amazon bestselling resource.

The Radical Acceptance Workbook

Transform Your Life & Free Your Mind with the Healing Power of Self-Love & Compassion — Positive Lessons to Treat Anxiety, Self-Doubt, Shame & Negative Self-Judgement

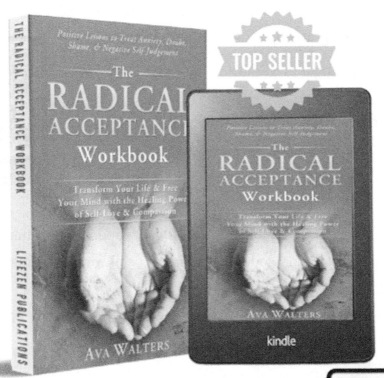

Click this link: https://life-zen.com/rad-acceptance
Or scan the QR code on this page.

Do You Have A Teenager?

If you do, help them happily, successfully, and safely
navigate TEEN LIFE with the…

DBT Skills Workbook for Teens

A Fun and Highly Relatable Workbook for Teens to Manage Difficult Emotions,
Cope with Teen Stress & Create Better Friendships

Includes 60+ Engaging Worksheets!

Click here to get your DBT copy now:
https://life-zen.com/dbt
Or scan the QR code on this page.

About the Author

Ava Walters is the founder of LifeZen Publications. Coming from a family with a history of mental health issues, her journey began as a personal quest to find balance, inner peace, and what we all desire—happiness. This pursuit has led her to explore traditional psychotherapeutic methods and diverse holistic practices.

She has an MBA with a specialization in International Project Management (IPM). However, her trajectory took a significant turn after experiencing "a burnout and a breakdown." She then returned to her first love—writing, complementing it with her deep passion for psychology. This transformation marked the beginning of her new journey. One focused on unraveling the intricate connections between human behavior and mental healing.

When she's not writing, Ava can be found on her yoga mat, taking long nature walks with her husband, or in the kitchen, constantly experimenting with new recipes to her husband's delight.

Learn more about Ava and LifeZen Publications here:
https://life-zen.com/

Index

Stress, 3, 4, 12, 14, 15, 20, 32, 39, 40, 44, 47, 48, 50, 60, 125, 148, 153

Struggles, 1, 4, 20, 59, 115, 123, 143

Surprise, 57

Trigger, 12, 40, 41, 52, 53, 54, 56, 78

Unhooking, 61, 116, 143

Values, 6, 13, 14, 15, 17, 24, 25, 53, 94, 95, 97, 99, 100, 101, 107, 108, 109, 110, 111, 115, 116, 117, 118, 119, 122, 123, 125, 127, 128, 129, 142, 144, 145, 146, 150

Values Bull's Eye, 112

Values clarification, 23, 24, 94, 149

Values-Based Exposure, 122

VBE, 122

Willingness, 15, 125

Worksheet

   Acknowledge, Allow, Accept, 34

   Box Breathing or Square Breathing, 46

   Closing Thought Tabs, 69

   Committed Action, 118

   Externalizing Thoughts, 72

   Grounding Using Your Five Senses, 49

   I Am..., 79

   I Want..., 21

   Kindness Mantras, 20

   Living in the Future, 126

   Mental Safe Space, 18

   Mindful Body Scan of Emotions, 59

   Mindful Walking in Nature, 48

   Name that Emotion, 54

   Non-Judgmental People Watching, 36

   Notice-Observe-Watch (NOW), 87

   Physical Safe Space, 16

References

1 Wikimedia Foundation. (2023, September 8). *Steven C. Hayes.* Wikipedia. https://en.wikipedia.org/wiki/Steven_C._Hayes

2 Öhman, A., & Mineka, S. (2001). Fears, phobias, and preparedness: Toward an evolved module of fear and Fear Learning. *Psychological Review, 108*(3), 483–522. https://doi.org/10.1037/0033-295x.108.3.483

3 Hasheminasab, M., Babapour Kheiroddin, J., Mahmood Aliloo, M., & Fakhari, A. (2015). Acceptance and Commitment Therapy (ACT) For Generalized Anxiety Disorder. Iranian journal of public health, 44(5), 718–719.

4 Eifert, G. H., Forsyth, J. P., Arch, J., Espejo, E., Keller, M., & Langer, D. (2009). Acceptance and commitment therapy for anxiety disorders: Three case studies exemplifying A unified treatment protocol. *Cognitive and Behavioral Practice, 16*(4), 368–385. https://doi.org/10.1016/j.cbpra.2009.06.001

5 Beygi, Z., Tighband Jangali, R., Derakhshan, N., Alidadi, M., Javanbakhsh, F., & Mahboobizadeh, M. (2023). An overview of reviews on the effects of acceptance and commitment therapy (ACT) on depression and anxiety. *Iranian Journal of Psychiatry.* https://doi.org/10.18502/ijps.v18i2.12373

6 Pohar, R., & Argáez, C. (2017, August 28). Acceptance and Commitment Therapy for Post-Traumatic Stress Disorder, Anxiety, and Depression: A Review of Clinical Effectiveness. Ottawa (ON): Canadian Agency for Drugs and Technologies in Health. Retrieved from https://www.ncbi.nlm.nih.gov/books/NBK525684/

7 Kelly, M. M., Reilly, E. D., Ameral, V., Richter, S., & Fukuda, S. (2022). A randomized pilot study of acceptance and commitment therapy to improve social support for veterans with PTSD. *Journal of Clinical Medicine, 11*(12), 3482. https://doi.org/10.3390/jcm11123482

8 Vakili, Y., & Gharraee, B. (2014). The effectiveness of acceptance and commitment therapy in treating a case of obsessive compulsive disorder. Iranian journal of psychiatry, 9(2), 115–117.

9 Soondrum, T., Wang, X., Gao, F., Liu, Q., Fan, J., & Zhu, X. (2022). The applicability of acceptance and commitment therapy for obsessive-compulsive disorder: A systematic review and meta-analysis. *Brain Sciences, 12*(5), 656. https://doi.org/10.3390/brainsci12050656

10 Osaji, J., Ojimba, C., & Ahmed, S. (2020). The use of acceptance and commitment therapy in Substance Use Disorders: A review of literature. *Journal of Clinical Medicine Research, 12*(10), 629–633. https://doi.org/10.14740/jocmr4311

11 Mosel, S. (2022, October 21). *Acceptance and commitment therapy (ACT) for substance abuse.* American Addiction Centers. https://americanaddictioncenters.org/therapy-treatment/act Reviewed by: Kristen Fuller, MD

12 Eklund, M., Kiritsis, C., Livheim, F., & Ghaderi, A. (2023). ACT-based self-help for perceived stress and its mental health implications without therapist support: A randomized controlled trial. *Journal of Contextual Behavioral Science, 27*, 98–106. https://doi.org/10.1016/j.jcbs.2023.01.003

13 Wersebe, H., Lieb, R., Meyer, A. H., Hofer, P., & Gloster, A. T. (2018). The link between stress, well-being, and psychological flexibility during an acceptance and commitment therapy self-help intervention. *International Journal of Clinical and Health Psychology*, *18*(1), 60–68. https://doi.org/10.1016/j.ijchp.2017.09.002

14 Feliu Soler, A., Montesinos, F., Gutiérrez-Martínez, O., Scott, W., McCracken, L., & Luciano, J. (2018). Current status of acceptance and commitment therapy for chronic pain: A narrative review. *Journal of Pain Research*, *Volume 11*, 2145–2159. https://doi.org/10.2147/jpr.s144631

15 Lai, L., Liu, Y., McCracken, L. M., Li, Y., & Ren, Z. (2023). The efficacy of acceptance and commitment therapy for chronic pain: A three-level meta-analysis and a trial sequential analysis of Randomized Controlled Trials. *Behaviour Research and Therapy*, *165*, 104308. https://doi.org/10.1016/j.brat.2023.104308

16 Pingo, J. C., Dixon, M. R., & Paliliunas, D. (2019). Intervention enhancing effects of acceptance and commitment training on performance feedback for direct support professional work performance, stress, and job satisfaction. *Behavior Analysis in Practice, 13*(1), 1–10. https://doi.org/10.1007/s40617-019-00333-w

17 Littlehales, N. (2024, February 1). *ACT as a workplace intervention: A path to employee well-being and performance.* Contextual Consulting. https://contextualconsulting.co.uk/mental-health/act-as-a-workplace-intervention-a-path-to-employee-well-being-and-performance

18 Fani Sobhani, F., Ghorban Shiroudi, S., & Khodabakhshi-Koolaee, A. (2021). Effect of two couple therapies, acceptance and commitment therapy and schema therapy, on forgiveness and fear of intimacy in conflicting couples.

Practice in Clinical Psychology, 9(4), 271–282. https://doi.org/10.32598/jpcp.9.4.746.3

19 Peterson, B. D., Eifert, G. H., Feingold, T., & Davidson, S. (2009). Using acceptance and commitment therapy to treat distressed couples: A case study with two couples. *Cognitive and Behavioral Practice, 16*(4), 430–442. https://doi.org/10.1016/j.cbpra.2008.12.009

20 Speedlin, S., Milligan, K., Haberstroh, S., & Duffey, T. (2016, September). Using acceptance and commitment therapy to negotiate losses and Life Transitions | Request PDF. https://www.researchgate.net/publication/327382040_Using_Acceptance _and_Commitment_Therapy_to_Negotiate_Losses_and_Life_Transitions

21 Hayes, S. C., Pistorello, J., & Levin, M. E. (2012). Acceptance and commitment therapy as a unified model of behavior change. *The Counseling Psychologist, 40*(7), 976–1002. https://doi.org/10.1177/0011000012460836

22 Zhang, C.-Q., Leeming, E., Smith, P., Chung, P.-K., Hagger, M. S., & Hayes, S. C. (2018). Acceptance and Commitment Therapy for Health Behavior Change: A contextually-driven approach. *Frontiers in Psychology, 8.* https://doi.org/10.3389/fpsyg.2017.02350

23 Ray, J. (2024, March 22). *World Unhappier, more stressed out than ever.* Gallup.com. https://news.gallup.com/poll/394025/world-unhappier- stressed-ever.aspx

24 Dochat, C., Wooldridge, J. S., Herbert, M. S., Lee, M. W., & Afari, N. (2021). Single-session acceptance and commitment therapy (ACT) interventions for patients with chronic health conditions: A systematic review and meta-

analysis. *Journal of Contextual Behavioral Science, 20,* 52–69. https://doi.org/10.1016/j.jcbs.2021.03.003

25 Ferreira, M. G., Mariano, L. I., Rezende, J. V., Caramelli, P., & Kishita, N. (2022). Effects of group acceptance and commitment therapy (ACT) on anxiety and depressive symptoms in adults: A meta-analysis. *Journal of Affective Disorders, 309,* 297–308. https://doi.org/10.1016/j.jad.2022.04.134

26 Schreuder, E., van Erp, J., Toet, A., & Kallen, V. L. (2016). Emotional responses to multisensory environmental stimuli. *SAGE Open, 6*(1), 215824401663059. https://doi.org/10.1177/2158244016630591

27 Dibdin, E. (2021, December 17). *How to connect with joy and happiness when you have depression.* Psych Central. https://psychcentral.com/depression/happy-when-depressed

28 Willroth, E. C., Young, G., Tamir, M., & Mauss, I. B. (2023). Judging emotions as good or bad: Individual differences and associations with psychological health. *Emotion, 23*(7), 1876–1890. https://doi.org/10.1037/emo0001220

29 Balban, M. Y., Neri, E., Kogon, M. M., Weed, L., Nouriani, B., Jo, B., Holl, G., Zeitzer, J. M., Spiegel, D., & Huberman, A. D. (2023). Brief structured respiration practices enhance mood and reduce physiological arousal. *Cell Reports Medicine, 4*(1), 100895. https://doi.org/10.1016/j.xcrm.2022.100895

30 Ewert, A., & Chang, Y. (2018). Levels of nature and stress response. *Behavioral Sciences, 8*(5), 49. https://doi.org/10.3390/bs8050049

31 Torre, J. B., & Lieberman, M. D. (2018). Putting feelings into words: Affect labeling as implicit emotion regulation. *Emotion Review, 10*(2), 116–124. https://doi.org/10.1177/1754073917742706

32 Wang, C., Schmid, C. H., Rones, R., Kalish, R., Yinh, J., Goldenberg, D. L., Lee, Y., & McAlindon, T. (2010). A randomized trial of Tai Chi for fibromyalgia. *New England Journal of Medicine, 363*(8), 743–754. https://doi.org/10.1056/nejmoa0912611

33 Tilbrook, H. E., Cox, H., Hewitt, C. E., Kang'ombe, A. R., Chuang, L.-H., Jayakody, S., Aplin, J. D., Semlyen, A., Trewhela, A., Watt, I., & Torgerson, D. J. (2011). Yoga for chronic low back pain. *Annals of Internal Medicine, 155*(9), 569. https://doi.org/10.7326/0003-4819-155-9-201111010-00003

34 Kan, L., Zhang, J., Yang, Y., & Wang, P. (2016). The effects of yoga on pain, mobility, and quality of life in patients with knee osteoarthritis: A systematic review. *Evidence-Based Complementary and Alternative Medicine, 2016*, 1–10. https://doi.org/10.1155/2016/6016532

35 Wu, Q., Liu, P., Liao, C., & Tan, L. (2022). Effectiveness of yoga therapy for Migraine: A meta-analysis of randomized controlled studies. *Journal of Clinical Neuroscience, 99*, 147–151. https://doi.org/10.1016/j.jocn.2022.01.018

36 Lee, A. (2020, April 7). *Why change is hard ... and good.* Columbia Business School. https://business.columbia.edu/cgi-leadership/ideas-work/why-change-hard-and-good

37 Call, M. (2024, April 15). *Why is behavior change so hard?*. Why is Behavior Change So Hard? https://accelerate.uofuhealth.utah.edu/resilience/why-is-behavior-change-so-hard

38 Harris, R. (2008). *The Happiness Trap*. Robinson.

39 Cascio, C. N., O'Donnell, M. B., Tinney, F. J., Lieberman, M. D., Taylor, S. E., Strecher, V. J., & Falk, E. B. (2015). Self-affirmation activates brain systems associated with self-related processing and reward and is reinforced by future orientation. *Social Cognitive and Affective Neuroscience, 11*(4), 621–629. https://doi.org/10.1093/scan/nsv136

Made in United States
North Haven, CT
13 March 2025

66777413R00096